DID YOU KNOW
YOU CAN TAKE ON THE CHALLENGE WITH YOUR WHOLE CHURCH?

ALL-IN, TURNKEY SERMON SERIES WITH PROVEN RESULTS!

WWW.REDLETTERGIVING.COM/CHURCH

WANT YOUR PASTOR TO RECEIVE A FREE COPY?
EMAIL HELLO@REDLETTERCHALLENGE.COM

Giving Challenge
Version 1.0

Copyright ©2025
Red Letter Living LLC
www.redlettergiving.com
www.redletterchallenge.com
hello@redletterchallenge.com

ALL RIGHTS RESERVED.

No part of this publication may be reproduced, stored, or transmitted in any form or by any means—for example, electronic, photocopy, or recording—without prior written permission. The only exception is brief quotations in printed reviews. Please encourage and participate in doing the right thing.

All Scripture quotations, unless otherwise noted, are taken from THE HOLY BIBLE, NEW INTERNATIONAL VERSION, NIV, Copyright 1973, 1978, 1984, 2011 by Biblica, Inc. Used by permission. All rights reserved worldwide.

Cover design and book layout by BlueLakeDesign.com.

Printed in the United States of America.

ACKNOWLEDGMENTS

Writing a book of this magnitude takes a team. It's one of life's greatest blessings to do meaningful work alongside people you genuinely care about.

Every time I write about Jesus, I fall more in love with Him. I continue to be astounded by His generosity. This book wouldn't exist if not for what Jesus has done—for everyone and personally for me.

To Allison—you are God's greatest earthly gift given to me. Thank you for being by my side through this entire journey. You are an incredible partner in both our family and ministry. I truly don't believe any of what we've created together would exist without your unwavering support and talent.

To our friends at the Quadrivium Group, Steve and Susan Blount—thank you for believing in our mission and helping move our projects forward. Doug Peterson, your masterful editing touches helped shape this work into its best form. Anne McLaughlin of Blue Lake Design, thank you for bringing our vision to life with creativity and excellence.

To those who reviewed this book and encouraged me through the process—Mama Z, JB, Hutton, GG, DHopp, Stephanie, and TP—your feedback was invaluable. Even more meaningful were the stories you shared about how this message inspired generosity in your own lives. That has deeply blessed me.

To the Red Letter Living team—especially Brenda and David—thank you for your steady, consistent work. You show up with excellence, again and again, and I'm so grateful for both of you.

Finally, to my son Nathan—or Nate-Dawg—I dedicate this book to you. While writing, I couldn't help but think of the incredible gift you are to me. At the time of this writing, you're just a year away from graduating and stepping into life's next big adventure. I believe in you. I know you have what it takes. And as God leads you into future success, my prayer is that you'll continue to live the generous life you've already begun so beautifully.

TABLE OF CONT

ACKNOWLEDGMENTS · · · · · · · · · 3

INTRO · · · · · · · · · · · · · · · 6
THE HEART OF THE MATTER

THE HEART OF THE MATTER
DAY 1: GIVING HAPPILY · · · · · · · · · 20
DAY 2: GIVING ETERNALLY · · · · · · · · 24
DAY 3: GIVING ABUNDANTLY · · · · · · · 28
DAY 4: GIVING REGULARLY · · · · · · · · 32
DAY 5: GIVING TODAY · · · · · · · · · · 38

GIVING HAPPILY
DAY 6 · · · · · · · · · · · · · · · 44
DAY 7 · · · · · · · · · · · · · · · 50
DAY 8 · · · · · · · · · · · · · · · 56
DAY 9 · · · · · · · · · · · · · · · 62
DAY 10 · · · · · · · · · · · · · · · 68
DAY 11 · · · · · · · · · · · · · · · 74
DAY 12 · · · · · · · · · · · · · · · 80

GIVING ETERNALLY
DAY 13 · · · · · · · · · · · · · · · 88
DAY 14 · · · · · · · · · · · · · · · 94
DAY 15 · · · · · · · · · · · · · · · 100
DAY 16 · · · · · · · · · · · · · · · 108
DAY 17 · · · · · · · · · · · · · · · 114
DAY 18 · · · · · · · · · · · · · · · 120
DAY 19 · · · · · · · · · · · · · · · 126

ENTS

GIVING ABUNDANTLY

DAY 20 · · · · · · · · · · · 134
DAY 21 · · · · · · · · · · · 140
DAY 22 · · · · · · · · · · · 146
DAY 23 · · · · · · · · · · · 152
DAY 24 · · · · · · · · · · · 158
DAY 25 · · · · · · · · · · · 164
DAY 26 · · · · · · · · · · · 170

GIVING REGULARLY

DAY 27 · · · · · · · · · · · 178
DAY 28 · · · · · · · · · · · 184
DAY 29 · · · · · · · · · · · 190
DAY 30 · · · · · · · · · · · 198
DAY 31 · · · · · · · · · · · 204
DAY 32 · · · · · · · · · · · 210
DAY 33 · · · · · · · · · · · 216

GIVING TODAY

DAY 34 · · · · · · · · · · · 224
DAY 35 · · · · · · · · · · · 230
DAY 36 · · · · · · · · · · · 236
DAY 37 · · · · · · · · · · · 244
DAY 38 · · · · · · · · · · · 250
DAY 39 · · · · · · · · · · · 256
DAY 40 · · · · · · · · · · · 262

DAY 41: THE FINAL CHALLENGE · · · · · · · 268

ABOUT THE AUTHOR · · · · · · · 272

ENDNOTES · · · · · · · · · · · 273

APPENDIX · · · · · · · · · · · 275

INTRODUCTION:
THE HEART OF THE MATTER

There I was, staring at the letter we'd received from our new neighbors right after moving into our first home. As I read the letter, I felt embarrassed, even like a failure.

The letter told me that my lawn did not meet the standards needed to live in this neighborhood. I glanced out my office window at the lawn and, sadly, couldn't argue. The Homeowner's Association (HOA) was right. My grass was a disaster. Not a speck of green, just an ugly mix of yellow and brown—two colors meant for bathroom toilets, not summer lawns.

The letter stated that I had one month to fix my lawn or else there would be more serious consequences. I was both angry and confused.

Three months prior, we had purchased our first home from a single man who kept his lawn in perfect, meticulous condition. In fact, if you were to look back at the records, you'd see his name as a multiple "Stoneybrook Hills Lawn of the Month" winner.

#GIVINGCHALLENGE

When I bought the home, I was determined to do everything possible to keep this high standard. I even dreamt early on of the day when, under my ownership, I'd see my first "Yard of the Month" sign. So, I spent time each week cutting and watering my grass. Doing all the things you need to do. And somehow, despite my best intentions and effort, I killed my yard.

Not only did the HOA not stick a winner sign in my yard, but it felt like they stuck a loser letter in my mailbox.

I couldn't figure out what was wrong with me.

Within a couple weeks of receiving the letter, I had to fork over more than $4,000 in brand-new St. Augustine sod. Talk about a gut-wrenching purchase.

I also learned later that in Florida you need to spray your yard with pesticides regularly. If you don't spray pesticides (and I didn't), then the insects, bugs, and pests will eat up your grass and totally destroy it. When you combine this with the fact that everyone else around me was spraying pesticides, all the grass-eating creatures in the entire city pretty much descended upon my yard. My grass became the delicacy for every pest in the city.

Once that chunk of cash left my bank account for new sod, something changed: I suddenly cared a lot about that grass. I checked on it multiple times a day. Once my money was in my sod, my heart was in it, too.

And not only my sod, but I also cared about everyone else's sod on the street. If I had to pay this much money for my grass, and if I'm being held to these standards, then everybody else better keep up their lawn as well, right? Through this unfortunate and crazy expensive lesson, I was reminded of a truth that Jesus once taught His disciples. He said in Matthew 6:21:

"FOR WHERE YOUR TREASURE IS, THERE YOUR HEART WILL BE ALSO."

Growing up in the Christian faith, I had heard this verse many times. I even had it memorized. Before you start thinking that's a big deal, it's only 11 words. It's not that hard to memorize. In fact, I bet if you stop right now and say it once or twice more, you'll already have it memorized.

More important than memorization, though, I have found out that when you apply the truth of this verse to your life, you stumble into experiencing three things nearly everyone chases but few find: significance, fulfillment, and joy.

The sod taught me an expensive truth that I could have just found in the red letters of Jesus. <u>Your money precedes your heart.</u>

This wasn't just true for me and my sod. I bet it is true for you too.

If you spend money to belong to a gym, your heart follows. You may even feel like you have a right to speak into the gym's overall vision or mission. Or maybe even on smaller things, like how the facilities are kept up.

If you save your money to spend on concert tickets, you expect a certain quality and experience.

It's the same if you buy stock for a company. The odds are that you didn't care about that company prior, but suddenly you have a vested interest. You care. You may go so far as to analyze the charts, set alerts or reminders on certain price points, or even review quarterly earnings.

"FOR WHERE YOUR TREASURE IS, THERE YOUR HEART WILL BE ALSO."

MATTHEW 6:21

#GIVINGCHALLENGE

Why is this?

Because you care about the things you pay for. You care about the people, the clubs, the events, or the companies you invest in.

So, what does this mean for those of us who believe in and follow Jesus? Many times I have heard from those who follow Jesus, "I just want a heart that beats for what God's heart beats for." Or "I want a heart that is more like God's." They are great statements. I also want that for myself. But, too often, when it comes to our money, we respond reactively, not proactively.

- What if the key to gaining a God-like heart is to first give of our money?
- What if we were generous *first* and then trusted that our hearts would automatically follow?

If you want a heart more like God's, then this is the book for you. But this will not be easy. Life's most significant challenges never come easy. But aren't you ready for something new? I bet you are.

Let me tell you why.

A SAD REALITY

Despite experiencing collective economic prosperity that is unrivaled in history, the average American Christian gives little to no more than the average non-Christian American.

In 2024, the average amount that Americans gave away was only 2.1 percent of the gross domestic product.[1] Christians give an average of 2.5 percent.[2] In other words, there is no discernible difference. Despite Jesus giving everything up for us, we collectively have become a nation of closed-fisted, stressed-out, grumpy hoarders. More than 6 out of 10 still self-profess a faith in Jesus Christ in America, yet collectively we give away $1 out of every $40 to $50 we make. That doesn't feel or sound like the generosity of Jesus.

It'd be one thing if we were doing all of this and experiencing a truly great life. You could kind of understand why we would choose this path if it were at least leading to a happy life. But it's not. We are living pretty miserable lives. As the famous rapper Notorious B.I.G. once said, "Mo' money, mo' problems." It shouldn't be that way. But somehow, it's become true.

If you are an average Christian in America today, you are experiencing more stress, burnout, loneliness, and mental unhealth than ever before.

The goal of this challenge is to fully give your heart to God, and that often starts with your finances. Money reveals our hearts, and for many of us, it exposes hidden idols. As Timothy Keller puts it, an idol is "anything that absorbs your heart and imagination more than God, or anything you seek to give you what only God can give."[3]

Money itself isn't evil; it's the love of it that's a root of all kinds of evil. So much of the evil that exists in our world today stems from money. Money isn't as much of an idol in and of itself, but it's the biggest revealer of idols in our lives.[4] What you do with your money shows what your heart truly longs for.

A significant part of this 40-day challenge will be trading in the false promises of money for the truths that lie in Jesus's teachings on generosity. Fair warning: I'm going to be stepping on some of your idols.

But again, I ask, aren't you ready for something new?

As we dive into the generosity of Jesus that He lived out and calls you to, you will be challenged to trade in your current relationship with money, guiding you toward a more generous life that reflects the heart of God. By intentionally examining where your "treasure" goes, you'll not only see your heart change but also discover a deeper sense of purpose, fulfillment, and joy.

While the book will focus on financial giving, the deeper purpose is for you to give your heart to God, which is ultimately what He wants most.

It won't be easy, but if you take this journey, you'll find it one of the most significant and fulfilling adventures of your life.

WHAT WILL THIS 40-DAY CHALLENGE LOOK LIKE?

The best place to learn how to be generous is to look at Jesus, the One who is the most generous. Over the next 40 days, as we embark on a journey to be generous like Jesus, we'll study His life and words. You'll also be invited into practical daily challenges to put His words into practice.

A follower of Jesus is someone who not only studies Jesus but does what He says to do. The words of Jesus were never meant to just stay red on a page or to only be lived out 2,000 years ago.

When you live out the words of Jesus today, you find the life you were made for.

Over the first days, you will examine the **HEART** of giving like Jesus. I'll share five powerful counter-cultural statements that Jesus delivered when it comes to living generously. As you read these introductory days, you'll also get a good roadmap of where you will be headed on this journey.

#GIVINGCHALLENGE

DAY 1: GIVING **H**APPILY:

"It is more blessed to give than to receive." **Acts 20:35b**

DAY 2: GIVING **E**TERNALLY:

"Life does not consist in an abundance of possessions." **Luke 12:15b**

DAY 3: GIVING **A**BUNDANTLY:

"For to whom much is given, much shall be required." **Luke 12:48b (RGT)**

DAY 4: GIVING **R**EGULARLY:

"You cannot serve both God and money." **Matthew 6:24b**

DAY 5: GIVING **T**ODAY:

"What good is it for someone to gain the whole world, yet forfeit their soul?" **Mark 8:36**

As we get into our weekly rhythms of *Giving Challenge*, on Days 6 to 40 you will explore how Jesus not only taught about generosity but also lived it out in every aspect of His life. Together, we'll uncover what opposes Jesus's teachings in today's world and learn how to counter these influences both with biblical truths and practical examples and tools. Through the rhythm of learning and practicing generosity, you'll be challenged to trade in the world's ideas about how to use money for the way of Jesus.

SO, WHAT ARE THE FIVE TRADES JESUS WILL CHALLENGE YOU TO MAKE?

DAYS 6-12

GIVING HAPPILY

TRADING COMFORT FOR CONTENTMENT

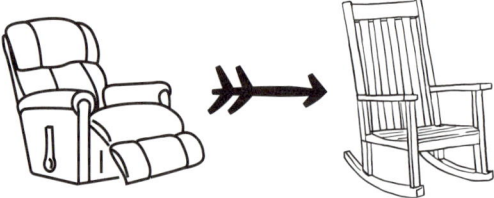

Rather than seeking comfort through money, you will discover that your true happiness comes from being content in who God is and what He's given to you.

DAYS 13-19

GIVING ETERNALLY

TRADING OWNERSHIP FOR STEWARDSHIP

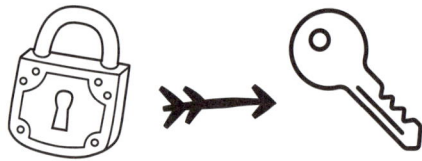

Rather than chasing after owning as much as humanly possible in the here and now, you will examine the truth that Heaven is our ultimate home, and all that you have now belongs to God.

#GIVINGCHALLENGE

DAYS 20-26
GIVING ABUNDANTLY

TRADING SCARCITY FOR ABUNDANCE

Rather than living with a scarcity mindset, you will be encouraged to live with an abundance mindset, knowing that the God you serve will supply all your needs.

DAYS 27-33
GIVING REGULARLY

TRADING CONTROL FOR OBEDIENCE

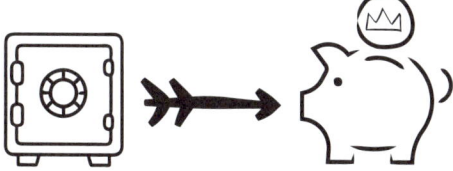

Rather than using your money to control as much as you can now, you will be challenged to obey God's commands by developing consistent, regular generosity habits.

DAYS 34-40
GIVING TODAY

TRADING GRASPING FOR GRATITUDE

Rather than grasping for more and more money, you will be encouraged to live with gratitude, remembering that God has and will give you everything you need.

None of these trades will be easy to make. They will press into and mess with your attitude, your mindset, and even your lifestyle. But the more trades you make, the more generous you will become.

THE MORE YOU LIVE AS JESUS CALLED YOU TO LIVE, THE HAPPIER YOU WILL BE.

A COUPLE OF BIG FAQ'S

1. ISN'T GIVING MORE THAN JUST ABOUT MONEY?

Yes, it is, but this book has a primary focus on our money or resources. Why? We've already written and discussed in detail what it looks like to give time and talent in our previous work, *Serving Challenge*.

To become the greatest disciples we can possibly be, we are hoping to be generous servants. This is a combination of giving time, talent, and certainly our treasure. While generosity is more than just giving money, it is not *less* than giving money. And for many of us, we have a harder time letting go of our money than we do of even our time or ability. We anticipate this challenge will stretch you in your faith, and ultimately that is our strongest aim for these next 40 days.

2. HOW MUCH ARE YOU CHALLENGING ME TO GIVE IN THIS 40-DAY CHALLENGE?

Through a combination of weekly challenges that will feature assessments, journaling, Scripture readings, guided prayer, and practical financial exercises, you will be challenged to give five gifts, one during each of the five weeks.

You will never be challenged to give a specific amount. A $10,000 gift might be a drop in a bucket for someone, while $100 could be someone else's entire bank account. We believe, first and foremost, that generosity flows from our relationship with God. The gifts will likely vary in size and scope, but we are praying that each one will be impactful and sacrificial.

One of the five gifts we are challenging you to give will not be a one-time gift, but rather a regular or recurring gift. This will happen on Days 27 to 33. Our hope is that through this book, your giving muscles can grow so you become the most generous person you can be.

I can't promise that if you complete the challenges you will have more money in your bank accounts by the time you finish, but I can promise this will be a joy-filled, happy, and fulfilling challenge to embark on. And that, friends, is worth more than any amount of money.

TIPS BEFORE YOU BEGIN

1. INVITE AN ALLY TO WALK WITH YOU.

Most of the greatest challenges that we conquer in life are not meant for individuals to tackle alone. Our hope is that you will do this challenge with at least one other person. If you are joining in this challenge with your small group or church, it's still important that you have one person who can help to hold you accountable for the duration of this challenge. This person should be someone you can trust deeply, is walking as a disciple of Jesus, and is mature in the faith. After finding an ally, identify specifics, such as how often you will check in with one another and what questions you will ask each other at those check-ins.

② TAKE THE FREE RED LETTER CHALLENGE ASSESSMENT.

Before you jump into *Giving Challenge*, spend seven to 10 minutes taking this FREE assessment. The online assessment was done in partnership with LifeWay Research and will measure how you are doing in your pursuit to follow Jesus. By doing this in advance, you'll have a greater understanding of how you can use these upcoming 40 days to grow in generosity just like Jesus. You can find the FREE assessment at
WWW.REDLETTERASSESSMENT.COM.

③ COMPLETE THE DAILY CHALLENGES.

After the first five introductory days, Days 6 to 40 offer a daily challenge to complete. Some of the challenges have an inner focus, while some have an external focus. To get the most out of this book, our hope is that you will take on the challenges in your own way. When it is an internal challenge, engage with the questions. Be honest with the personal reflections and write down your responses. When it is an external challenge, even if it takes you out of your comfort zone, try your best to physically complete the challenge.

④ DON'T GIVE UP.

You will not do this challenge perfectly. Give yourself grace. This challenge goes beyond checking boxes just to get it done. It will give you the opportunity to put your beliefs into actions. We have found that the most vulnerable day, the day you're tempted to give up, is "the day after perfect." If you miss a day or struggle with a day, don't give up. Instead, give yourself grace and pick up the next day. Keep walking.

#GIVINGCHALLENGE

5 **SHARE THE WINS.**

Join the thousands of others embarking on the journey. Use **#GIVINGCHALLENGE** at any time on social media to share pictures, quotes, stories, or testimonies of what God is doing in your story. Sharing your wins publicly will not only encourage others to do the same, but it will also give people the opportunity to glorify God through your generosity.

THE 40-DAY GIVING CHALLENGE IS ON!

DAY 1
GIVING HAPPILY

> **"It is more blessed to give than to receive."**
> **Acts 20:35b**

In their book *Happy Money*, authors Elizabeth Dunn and Michael Norton look at the science of how we use our money today, and they report some important discoveries. Here's one of their key findings: "New research demonstrates that spending money on others provides a bigger happiness boost than spending money on yourself."[5]

Sometimes I laugh at how long it takes for science to catch up to God.

There are only a few words of Jesus outside of the Gospels of Matthew, Mark, Luke, and John. So, when you see them in your Bible, they truly jump off the page. One of those instances is in the 20th chapter of the book of Acts. The apostle Paul is saying his final goodbyes to his friends from Ephesus and giving them some departing words. In the midst of this, he gives us this gem from Jesus in Acts 20:35b:

> **"It is more blessed to give than to receive."**

The word "blessed" in the Greek is best translated as "most happy." Fortunate. Well off. Once again, science confirms what Jesus taught us long ago!

Jean Twenge, American psychologist, has studied mental health and happiness in our nation. She writes, "By most accounts, Americans should be happier now than ever. The violent crime rate is low, as is the unemployment rate. Income per capita has steadily grown over the last few decades . . . As the standard of living improves, so should happiness—but it has not."[6]

While Twenge would go on to talk about multiple factors, emphasizing the role of digital media on our happiness levels, I think the lie most of us believe is that if we increase our standard of living, then we will automatically be happier. We believe that the more we have, the more comfortable we will be, and the greater happiness we will have.

Jesus's message, now echoed by science, reveals that true happiness isn't found in raising our standard of living but in elevating our standard of giving.

This may not be as crazy as you think. What's true for America is also true for the rest of the world.

> "In 120 out of 136 countries, people who donated to charity in the past month reported greater satisfaction with life . . . Across the 136 countries studied in the Gallup World Poll, donating to charity had a similar relationship to happiness as doubling household income."[7]

Can I be honest with you? If you want to be happy, isn't it so much easier to donate some money than it is to attempt to double your household income?

So, what do you say? Are you ready for an adventure where we will attempt to raise your standard of giving so that in the end you can actually have a more satisfying, meaningful, and happier life?

But is it okay to pursue happiness?

AN ODD RELATIONSHIP WITH HAPPINESS

I have found that American Christians have an odd relationship with the word "happy." In one sense, we protect our right to pursue happiness and are extremely proud to have it listed in some of the first words of our Declaration of Independence.

> "We hold these truths to be self-evident, that all men are created equal, that they are endowed by their Creator with certain unalienable Rights, that among these are Life, Liberty and the pursuit of Happiness."[8]

Did you notice that the Declaration even says the pursuit of happiness flows from our Creator? So, in one breath we want to protect this right as an American citizen. But then, as an American Christian, we will go to church and hear many of our pastors say something catchy and sticky like this: "God cares more about your holiness than your happiness."

When they say things like this, it's a confusing message for sure. So, which is it? Are we to pursue happiness? Or is holiness the best pursuit? I 100-percent agree that God cares about your holiness. When the pastor says a phrase like this, the pastor is pointing out how important holiness is in the world today. We still desperately need to hear the message of holiness in a world that tolerates and normalizes unholiness.

But make no mistake about it. God also cares about your happiness.

Can't Jesus be for your happiness *and* your holiness?

This might surprise you, but did you know that in the first 14 verses of the words of Jesus, He says the word "happy" nine times?[9] Jesus is ridiculously and utterly committed to bringing to you a life of happiness. A happy life is literally the first main idea that Jesus presents, and it's recorded over and over for us.

Everything Jesus did, and everything He gave, was ultimately so we could experience eternal happiness right now. His Kingdom is a Happy Kingdom.

When you look at the life and words of Jesus, we will see that holiness and happiness go together. We ought not call people to holiness at the expense of happiness. The more we pursue Jesus and put His words into practice (i.e. holiness), the happier we will be.

Please don't misunderstand. To be happy, truly happy, is not the same as a comfortable life. Happy and comfortable are not synonyms. They never have been and never will be. I would argue that the pursuit of a comfortable life is not ultimately satisfying. God created us with special gifts and the power and authority to do hard things, to live with significance, to steward this Earth, and to bring God's coming Kingdom to the here and now. Truly living like Jesus is not comfortable, but it is far better than the alternative.

So, let's embrace the truth that Jesus's call to holiness and His promise of happiness are not at odds. When we live out His words and embody the way He lived, especially through generous giving, we step into a life that is both holy and happy—a holy happiness you might say.

On Days 6-12, we'll explore contentment, which is the healthy attitude underneath the generous life that Jesus invites us into. Giving like Jesus must begin with our attitude.

This week, we will focus on the attitude of Jesus and how His happiness came from knowing that the generous price He paid would lead to a relationship with you. His sacrifice was worth it! During this week, you'll be challenged to break free from using your money and resources to maximize your comfort in this world and instead choose to live with contentment no matter what comes your way.

Finally, you'll be invited to "Give a Happy Gift" this week.

DAY 2

GIVING ETERNALLY

> "Life does not consist in an abundance of possessions."
> Luke 12:15b

A Russian missionary who visited America was once asked by a pastor, "What is it you see in our country, of those who claim faith in Jesus, that is inconsistent with God's Word?" He was essentially trying to figure out what, if any, blind spots exist among American Christians.

It didn't take him long to respond. Without hesitation, the missionary responded with two words, "Public storage."

The missionary went on to explain how many Americans have so much stuff that no longer fits in their houses, closets, or garages. A good percentage of those people pay a monthly rental fee to a storage unit facility just to keep all their extra stuff. Finally, he said that while America is a nation that is a certain percentage Catholic, a certain percentage Protestant, etc., it is a 100-percent materialistic nation.[10]

Just a quick Google search will show you how much Americans love their stuff. The public storage industry has grown over the past 40 years from 6,600 to more than 50,000 units and is statistically growing faster than the music, entertainment, and travel industries. U.S. storage facilities represent more than 90 percent of all the storage facilities in the world.[11]

Is the Russian missionary right? Do many of us have an unhealthy relationship with our stuff? Getting more personal, do you have an unhealthy relationship with your stuff?

JESUS SAID WHAT?

Believe it or not, Jesus isn't silent on the topic of self-storage. Jesus was once asked a question that sparked a story. It's found in Luke 12:13-21.

> **Someone in the crowd said to him,** "Teacher, tell my brother to divide the inheritance with me."
>
> **Jesus replied,** "Man, who appointed me a judge or an arbiter between you?" **Then he said to them,** "Watch out! Be on your guard against all kinds of greed; life does not consist in an abundance of possessions."
>
> **And he told them this parable:** "The ground of a certain rich man yielded an abundant harvest. He thought to himself, 'What shall I do? I have no place to store my crops.'
>
> "Then he said, 'This is what I'll do. I will tear down my barns and build bigger ones, and there I will store my surplus grain. And I'll say to myself, "You have plenty of grain laid up for many years. Take life easy; eat, drink and be merry."'
>
> "But God said to him, 'You fool! This very night your life will be demanded from you. Then who will get what you have prepared for yourself?'
>
> "This is how it will be with whoever stores up things for themselves but is not rich toward God."

Jesus calls those who live for the purpose of more self-storage in this world "fools." The actual Greek word for fool, *"aphros,"* implies stupid, ignorant, and unbelieving. Too strong?

He then reminds all of those who are listening that each one of our lives has an expiration date. We don't know when our last day on this Earth will be. It's important for me to acknowledge, of course, that it is difficult to prioritize our heavenly future over our earthly one. As Christians, 100 percent of our existence has been on Earth; so it's much easier and more natural for us to think and understand what we know today versus the unknown reality of Heaven.

Despite this, Jesus still makes this point loud and clear: <u>Fools live more for today than eternity.</u>

Yet, many of us have this backwards. We spend more of our time building our own kingdom rather than building God's Kingdom.

In fact, let me bust a myth that you may have heard before.

Some will tell you the thing Jesus talked about most is money. Well, actually, that's not true. To be fair, He did talk a lot about money. But He talked about His Kingdom even more than about money. Oftentimes, when Jesus does talk about money, like in the parable above, the main point is not actually about money, but points to something else.

The above story doesn't say storage is wrong. Or even that it's bad to have things. The story reminds us of a heavenly Kingdom that is coming for those who believe in Jesus.

And if that heavenly Kingdom is coming, it's foolish to spend your time-stamped years on this Earth living for stuff that has an expiration date and will eventually rot and decay. Jesus invites us who believe in Him over and over again to see this life through the lens of His Kingdom. When we look at our lives with this lens, we move away from the desire to own as much as possible and instead learn to steward all things.

Trading the idea of *owning* everything to *stewarding* all things will lead not only to a more generous life, but a happier life.

#GIVINGCHALLENGE

If you say you believe in and trust Jesus, then part of our rhythm as His followers is to regularly think and imagine what Heaven will one day be like. This practice will help us to remember that Heaven is real and everything we do for God's Kingdom now will somehow, in some way, make our eternal future that much greater.

The generous sacrifice of Jesus tells us that the most valuable aspect of God's Kingdom is not material things, but people. When you invest in the lives of people today, you invest in the Kingdom of God.

Imagine standing before God one day, with everything you've accumulated and left behind, and realizing you could have built something far greater with Him. What kingdom have you truly invested in?

On Days 13-19, we will explore how to give and use our resources with an eternal perspective. God is not against you having nice things. But He is against you living for anything other than His Kingdom. When your money or your stuff gets in the way of your relationship with God, or takes precedence over everything else, you need a relationship shift with money.

During this week, we will flip the perspective that many of us have when it comes to our money. Rather than living like an owner, you'll be challenged to live more like a steward.

As you learn to live by this new perspective, you'll be continually reminded that as great as this world is, Heaven is greater. You only get one life right now on this Earth, so let's use it to make God's Kingdom that much bigger and better. During this week, you'll be challenged to give a gift that can truly make an eternal impact.

DAY 3

GIVING ABUNDANTLY

> "For to whom much is given, much shall be required."
> Luke 12:48b (RGT)

Give What We Can estimates that, even considering the cost of living, you may be wealthier than you think. Earning $31,300 places you in the global top 5 percent of wage earners. At $40,000, you are in the top 3 percent, $47,000 puts you in the top 2 percent, and $60,000 makes you part of the top 1 percent.

Curious about your own rank? Visit www.givingwhatwecan.org to see exactly where you stand. Understanding where you are financially helps you better steward God's blessings.

If you are financially rich and a believer in Jesus, you should not only feel incredibly grateful for God's provision, but you should also have a sense of great responsibility to use your dollars and resources to right things that are wrong in this world.

That is what Jesus says in Luke 12:48b (RGT): **"For to whom much is given, much shall be required."**

If those who are rich simply stepped up and donated a small portion of their fortune, so much of the poverty and injustices of the world could be changed. Did you know that if the top 1 percent of wage earners in the world donated 10 percent of their income, there would be an estimated 3.6 trillion dollars given overall to charity?

Here are a few things that could happen with that 3.6 trillion dollars:

1. End extreme poverty for a year (estimated $256 billion)
2. Clean water and sanitation for all, once and for all (estimated $1.22 trillion)
3. End hunger and malnutrition (estimated $341 billion)

Not only could we meet tangible needs, but that would leave us another 2 trillion dollars to take care of other things, like spiritual needs.[12] If you take the average cost to plant a new church in America (which is higher than nearly any other country), that 2 trillion dollars would help plant more than 6 million churches.[13]

Those are all things we could do with just the top 1 percent. Can you imagine how many wrongs would be made right if all believers, not just the richest ones, were to give away 10 percent or more of their income?

If you are an American Christian, you live in a nation of abundance, and yet, for many of you, you still don't feel rich.

FEELINGS AREN'T ALWAYS TRUE

If you don't feel wealthy, consider why.

Possible reasons include being constantly exposed to richer lifestyles, always knowing someone who has more, desiring more, falling for clever marketing, and believing that products you don't own will somehow solve your problems.

Any therapist worth their salt will remind you that while your feelings may be real, they are not always true.

You can be rich but still not *feel* rich.

The overarching reason many of us don't feel rich, however, comes down to our mindset. Name as many reasons or excuses as you want for not feeling rich, but it all boils down to how you view the world.

There are two opposing ways to see the world: a scarcity mindset or an abundance mindset.

A scarcity mindset is a way of thinking that focuses on what you lack or don't have enough of. It can lead to conserving, hoarding, self-preservation, and competition. If there's only a certain amount of resources available, then you need to do everything you possibly can to take care of yourself. The more you operate with a scarcity mindset, the more challenging it will be to live generously.

An abundance mindset is a way of thinking that focuses on what you have and recognizes there are more than enough resources available. It can lead to gratitude, contentment, and collaboration. The more you operate with an abundance mindset, the more open you will be to living generously.

The more you listen to the world or the lies of the enemy, you will be consumed by a scarcity mindset. The more you listen to the truth of the Gospel, you will be filled with an abundance mindset. So, if you want to look at the world with an abundance mindset, continue to listen to God's truth more than the lies of the enemy.

When you hear God's truth, you'll be reminded that He is the Good Shepherd who gives you everything you need. With Him watching over you, like David says in Psalm 23:1, you lack nothing. He delights in providing for you. The One who created the world and owns all the resources of the world loves you. Of course, He will take good care of you.

He has already! Jesus held nothing back when He spilled His entire life for you and for me on the cross. Every act of generosity that we perform in this world is in response to Jesus's abundant gift to us. If He gave that for us, who are we to hoard and hold back?

On Days 20-26, we will look at how God has abundantly loved and given to us. Spiritually speaking, you are filthy rich, and financially speaking, many who are reading this are also filthy rich. We will look at what is required, commanded, and expected for those of us who are in Christ Jesus.

You will also learn how to let go of the scarcity mindset so you can fully adopt an abundance mindset. Finally, in response to God's abundance of blessings for you, you will be challenged to give out of your abundance of resources this week.

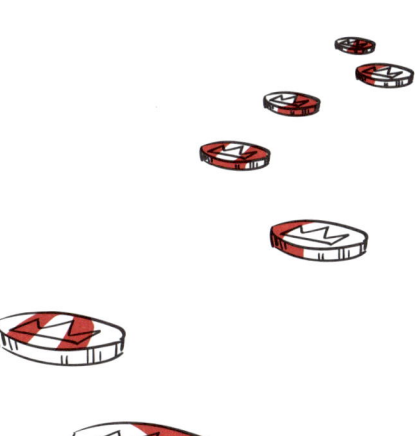

DAY 4

GIVING REGULARLY

> "You cannot serve both God and money."
> **Matthew 6:24b**

It's time for an idol hunt. But don't worry, this isn't *Survivor*, and you're not getting voted off any island. This hunt is more important because these idols don't just affect a game; they shape our entire lives.

Jesus once said, "You cannot serve both God and money." But don't we often feel like we can be the exception? We think, "I can serve God *and* make all the money I want." Or "Once God blesses me with money, I'll be one of the most generous people ever." Sound familiar? I've thought it and probably even said it out loud.

But no matter how much money you have, here's the truth:

Money is a terrible master, but it makes a terrific servant.

Money itself isn't evil; it's the *love* of it that's a root of all kinds of evil. And as we've already mentioned in the introduction, money isn't an idol in itself, but it's the biggest revealer of idols in our lives. What we do with our money shows what our hearts truly value.

The problem is that we often don't want to admit what our financial habits might reveal. If we were to take a hard look at our financial statements, we might find that what we treasure most isn't God's Kingdom, but the pursuit of comfort, security, or status—all things that can easily become idols. And that's exactly why you will go on an idol hunt in this book.

What does your money reveal about your heart? This isn't just a theoretical exercise. How we spend, save, or give money shows what we truly worship. Take about 10 minutes now to review your financial accounts, your net worth, and your last month of purchases. Reflect on what you see. Does your money—how much you have or where you are spending it—reveal an idol in your life?

- Do you see 10 different streaming service platforms you pay for? Maybe entertainment or pleasure is your idol.

- Do you hoard money in savings but hesitate to bless others because "something might happen"? Maybe fear or control is your idol.

- Do you own a closet full of clothes, shoes, and accessories—many of which you rarely wear? Maybe image or status is your idol.

- Do you drop large amounts of money on experiences—travel, concerts, amusement parks—but struggle to give consistently? Maybe adventure or excitement is your idol.

What idol or potential idols does your money reveal in your life?

_____

_____

_____

Here's the good news: We're not just here to expose the idols in our lives; we're here to replace them with something infinitely better—Jesus Himself. No matter what your past has looked like, Jesus invites you to follow Him. The key to replacing an idol isn't removing money from the picture entirely, because money itself isn't inherently bad. Instead, it's learning to use money the way God intended—as a tool to fulfill His purposes.

FROM BELIEF TO OBEDIENCE

Belief in Jesus is foundational to our faith. But there's a vast difference between believing in Him and following Him. To follow Jesus means more than acknowledging Him as Savior. It means letting Him be Lord over every area of our lives, including our finances. This is where the practice of obedience comes in.

Obedience isn't a burden; it's the natural outflow of genuine faith. And, more so, it's the test of whether we truly love Jesus. In John 14:15, Jesus said, **"If you love me, keep my commands."** When we truly follow Jesus, we begin to align our actions with His teachings, particularly in how we use our resources. The way we use our money is both a practical and spiritual issue.

Thankfully, Jesus talked a lot about money. Why? Because people desperately need wisdom when it comes to their finances. One of the wisest things you need to hear again today is to not be just like everyone else when it comes to how you spend your money.

Here's what's normal for many of us when it comes to finances, even in times of prosperity:

- Financial stress
- Living paycheck to paycheck with no margin
- Monthly debt payments
- Worry, anxiety, and fear
- Tension in our relationships
- Fights in our marriages

That is one reason why Jesus is calling you to not be normal, because normal is not working.

#GIVINGCHALLENGE

MONEY IS A
TERRIBLE MASTER,
BUT IT MAKES
A TERRIFIC
SERVANT.

#GIVINGCHALLENGE

You can stop being controlled by your money and instead you can control your money. How you control your money, or use your money, if you are truly following Jesus, must start with obedience.

GENEROSITY HABITS

If our money can reveal our hearts, is it possible that the way we treat and use money could reveal our hearts to be pure and God-focused? What would it look like to use money in a way that reveals God? The answer, of course, is to become generous in seeing God's Kingdom come to reality in this world. When you give toward God's mission, you reveal that money does not have power over you and that God is at the throne of your heart.

Now, here's the thing: Giving a sacrificial gift once or twice is definitely worth celebrating. You will be encouraged to do that in this 40-day challenge. However, a one-time action isn't enough to uproot and replace an idol. So, how do you get rid of idols? Some say you can't just remove idols, but you can *replace* them.

Replacing idols requires consistency and regularity. Generosity is more than a one-time event or gift; it is a life marked by consistent habits. From the beginning of creation, God emphasized giving from our firstfruits, not our leftovers, and regularly practicing the tithe—principles that are deeply woven into His design for our lives. Generosity doesn't just combat the idol of money; it actively shifts our hearts and priorities back to God's Kingdom.

Look at Jesus as the perfect example. God so loved the world that He gave us Jesus, His first and only begotten son. And Jesus so loved the world that He gave us everything He had, including His very life. In Him, we see the ultimate picture of giving firstfruits, even if it means sacrifice and personal cost. And yes, Jesus did speak about tithing—just once—but in that one mention, He affirmed it. He reminded His followers that tithing was good, but He also made it clear not to neglect justice, mercy, and faithfulness (Matthew 23:23).

When we give regularly in the way that Jesus asks us to, when we choose to put God's mission before our own comforts or desires, we reveal that money no longer has dominion over us. Instead, we show that God is the true ruler of our hearts.

While obedience to these habits should be embraced and expected, it's fair to point out that it's not the norm today for most Christians. Imagine the difference we could make if we all stepped into obediently living out Jesus's words. The world would be radically different. Getting these habits into our lives is a worthy starting point in a life of generosity.

On Days 27-33, we're going to explore how to make generosity not just a one-time act, but an obedient lifestyle. I'll challenge you to get into the rhythm of regular giving by practicing generosity habits so that your heart can be fully surrendered to God through your finances. Giving regularly is the way we can start replacing the things that try to control us with the only One truly worthy of our hearts.

It's the way we ensure that money remains a servant and doesn't become our master.

DAY 5

GIVING TODAY

> "What good is it for someone to gain the whole world, yet forfeit their soul?"
> Mark 8:36

Let's start with an honest question: How often do you chase after things you think will make you happy? A better job, a bigger house, more money, or higher status? The world promises fulfillment if you just get "this," whatever "this" might be. But once you have it, the feeling doesn't last. You still want more.

The world of collectibles went crazy during the Covid-19 pandemic, and no, I'm not just talking about buying every single roll of toilet paper off the shelves. For many, collectibles blur the line between hobbies and investments. For me, collectibles, though seemingly harmless, have revealed how easily my heart can stray in the wrong direction.

As a kid, opening packs of sports cards in search of a star rookie was the highlight of my birthdays. The thrill of chasing and finding limited-edition or rare items stayed with me into adulthood. In my 20s and 30s, I ran an online business selling golf headcovers. I became an expert in spotting deals, especially Scotty Cameron headcovers, the most prized of all. At first, it was fun to buy low and sell high. But soon, I wasn't just selling. I was collecting. The more I had, the more I wanted.

Each new headcover brought a rush of excitement. But after unboxing it, I'd toss it in a drawer and start chasing the next one. My collection grew, but I was never fully satisfied. I now look back on that season with regret, wondering if I could have made a larger difference using my money in different ways. I learned the hard way that living for "more" doesn't ever satisfy. It only traps you in an endless cycle.

The Bible calls this greed, and it isn't just about money. It's a subtle force that promises happiness but delivers emptiness. Advertisements tell us the next purchase will complete us. Social media suggests one more achievement will bring fulfillment. But even celebrities with fame and fortune struggle with emptiness, proving worldly things can't fill a God-shaped void.

WHEN THINGS BECOME IDOLS

It's not wrong to have hobbies or collections. But when those things take the number-one place in your heart, they become idols, and you are in jeopardy of violating the very first commandment to "have no other gods" before Him (Exodus 20:3).

I knew my collection was a problem when I woke up thinking about an auction ending later that night, which would give me the chance to get the headcover I had been chasing. When I was thinking more about golf headcovers in the morning than about the very God of the universe, I knew that somehow, golf headcovers, the silliest of things, had become my idol.

In the Old Testament, I used to think the Israelites were crazy for worshiping idols like golden calves or household gods. How could they replace God with objects? But then I realized my golf headcovers were just my own 21st-century way of living out this sin. The headcovers were literally just sitting on a shelf, or inside a drawer, and they were taking over my heart. What ridiculousness!

Greed can spiral out of control before you know it. Something innocent can take hold of you until it consumes your thoughts and priorities. Whenever we let anything replace God in our hearts, we lose. Jesus warned us in Mark 8:36:

"What good is it for someone to gain the whole world, yet forfeit their soul?"

Even if we could achieve everything the world offers, it would mean nothing if we lose the core of who we are, our eternal soul.

To "forfeit" means to give something up entirely. If you forfeit, you cannot win—it's impossible. Jesus says it's possible to win the whole wide world and still lose because you've given up your soul. Chasing after the world's rewards at the expense of your soul is a tragic trade.

Jesus's question forces us to evaluate our priorities. What are we trading for temporary gains? Are we neglecting our spiritual lives for material success? Are we building earthly kingdoms, which are temporary, while ignoring God's Kingdom, which is eternal?

LIVING AS CONDUITS, NOT CONTAINERS

Every soul longs to connect with its Creator. Augustine put it perfectly: "You have made us for Yourself, O Lord, and our hearts are restless until they rest in You." That restlessness drives us to seek fulfillment, but when we turn to created things instead of the Creator, we end up unsatisfied.

The best way to combat greed is by living with gratitude. Greed always wants more, but gratitude celebrates what we already have. Gratitude naturally leads to generosity, creating a cycle of receiving blessings from God and passing them on to others.

When it comes to God's blessings, you can choose to live as a container or a conduit. Containers collect and store things, while conduits let blessings flow through them. Too often, we live like containers, holding onto everything we can.

Our containers can get bigger and fancier, yet many who live this way still feel stressed. Conduits, on the other hand, receive from God and pass His blessings to others. This is how Jesus lived, and it's how we're designed to live too.

Jesus challenges us to consider what we're living for. When you look at all His red letters, Jesus spoke more about giving than saving, planning, or investing. While those things have their place, generosity truly reflects the heart of God. Living as conduits means that you actively share God's blessings every day. When God is first in your life, gratitude overflows, and you can't help but be a conduit and share what He's given you to others.

A life of gratitude not only remembers how God has provided for you but also inspires you to help others experience His gifts too. You find that you weren't created to hoard God's blessings. You were made to share them. When you let His generosity flow through you, you may have less of the world's possessions, but you'll have more of what truly matters.

During Days 34-40, we'll explore practical ways to bless others daily. We get the opportunity to be generous every single day, and you will be challenged to not only look for opportunities to be generous but to act on them.

Just as Jesus poured out His life for us, we are called to pour out His blessings into the lives of others. Imagine the impact if we all lived as conduits, reflecting God's heart and sharing His blessings every day. True generosity isn't about what we store up. It's about freely giving away to others what God has first given to you.

DAYS 6-12

OF THE 40-DAY CHALLENGE

WEEK 2:

GIVING HAP

TRADING COMFORT FOR CONTENTMENT

"It is more blessed to give than to receive."

Acts 20:35b

DAY 6

THE WORST SOUP-ER BOWL EVER

> "Man shall not live on bread alone, but on every word that comes from the mouth of God."
>
> **Matthew 4:4**

Life is full of trades, some better than others. In football, for example, trades can define a team's future. Just ask any Cleveland Browns fan about the blockbuster deal for quarterback Deshaun Watson. Three years and $230 million later, it's already been deemed the worst trade in NFL history. As a Browns fan, it's painful to watch our team rebuilding yet again, while the team we traded with thrives. Being a Browns fan is miserable.

But bad trades aren't limited to football. Every day, we make trades in our own lives. We exchange health for junk food, time with loved ones for mindless distractions, and long-term goals for fleeting pleasures. These trades often feel absurd in hindsight, but they reflect a deeper truth about human nature: We often choose temporary comfort over lasting contentment. Perhaps no story illustrates this more powerfully than Esau's, who traded his birthright for a bowl of vegetable stew.

In Genesis 25, we meet Esau, the firstborn son of Isaac. As the firstborn, Esau had a birthright, a double portion of his father's inheritance and the privilege of carrying the family legacy. Yet, in a moment of hunger, he traded it all for a bowl of vegetable stew.

Here's how the story unfolds:

> **Once when Jacob was cooking some stew, Esau came in from the open country, famished. He said to Jacob, "Quick, let me have some of that red stew! I'm famished!"**
>
> **Jacob replied, "First, sell me your birthright."**
>
> **"Look, I am about to die," Esau said. "What good is the birthright to me?" Genesis 25:29-30a, 31-32**

Esau exaggerated his hunger, dismissed the value of his birthright, and chose immediate comfort over lasting contentment. Jacob gives Esau some lentil stew, and then, tragically, Scripture says:

> **He ate and drank, and then got up and left. So Esau despised his birthright. Genesis 25:34b**

Esau's story highlights a critical truth: When we focus on immediate needs, we risk forfeiting what matters most. Choosing comfort in the moment often costs us the deep contentment that comes from living as a follower of Jesus. Ten minutes of lentil decadence cost him decades of the life God had intended for him.

Esau's bowl of veggies might not tempt us, but we face decisions every day that challenge our priorities. How often do we trade what truly matters for fleeting comfort?

QUICK TRADES

In today's culture of instant gratification, these trades are more tempting and easier to make than ever. Whether it's mindlessly scrolling through social media, bingeing on unhealthy food, or chasing material possessions, we're surrounded by "bowls of stew" that promise immediate comfort. Yet these choices often leave us feeling empty and disconnected, robbing us of the lasting joy and contentment found in Christ.

Esau's story feels absurd. After all, who trades something so valuable for stew, especially stew that doesn't even have a chunk of meat in it?

But when we examine our lives, we see similar patterns. While Esau reached for a bowl of stew, we might reach for a short-term distraction—a certain product, luxury, or experience that we can have right now instead of choosing the deeper satisfaction of trusting God. All it takes is just one swipe of the credit card and we can have immediate pleasure.

Hunger of any kind often drives impulsive decisions. Like grocery shopping on an empty stomach leads to junk food, an empty soul seeks anything to fill the void, even things that harm us or distract us from the life God calls us to live.

Esau's hunger wasn't just physical; it reflected a deeper emptiness. Consumed by his immediate need, he lost sight of his greater blessing. Similarly, when we focus on temporary comfort, we risk forgetting God's eternal promises.

In Matthew 4:4, Jesus said, **"Man shall not live on bread alone, but on every word that comes from the mouth of God."** Staying spiritually nourished through God's Word helps us choose contentment over fleeting comforts.

When you are in the presence of God, you lack nothing. You do not walk around hungry or craving anything because you realize He has given you everything you need. Contentment comes from trusting that God has, is, and will provide everything you need. His promises are better than any temporary things the world can offer. Contentment allows us to say "no" to quick fixes because we know something better is coming.

Esau didn't have this perspective. He saw only his immediate hunger and lost sight of the greater blessing his birthright represented. When we focus on God's promises instead of our temporary discomfort, we can avoid making the same mistake.

#GIVINGCHALLENGE

LOSING AND GAINING OUR BIRTHRIGHT

Esau's birthright represented his identity, inheritance, and future. By trading it for a bowl of stew, he gave up something irreplaceable. His story mirrors ours. Like Esau, we've all traded our birthright, our identity in Christ, for the fleeting pleasures of sin. Romans 3:23 reminds us, **". . . for all have sinned and fall short of the glory of God."**

Sin is the ultimate bad trade. It promises satisfaction but leaves us empty. It offers quick fixes but results in long-term loss. And like Esau, we often walk away feeling unhappy, wondering why we gave up so much for so little.

But here's the good news: Jesus didn't make the same mistake.

Unlike Esau, Jesus didn't trade His birthright for a quick fix. Jesus, the ultimate firstborn Son, didn't take the bowl. In Romans 8:29, Jesus is called the "firstborn among many brothers and sisters." Instead of choosing comfort, He chose contentment in God's plan, even when it meant enduring the discomfort of the cross.

Where Esau failed, Jesus succeeded. Where we traded our birthright, Jesus preserved His, and then He gave it up for us. Through His death and resurrection, Jesus offers to restore what we've lost. Jesus didn't just die for us. He rose again to give us a new identity. John 1:12 says, **"Yet to all who did receive him, to those who believed in his name, he gave the right to become children of God."**

You're no longer a starving wanderer. You're a son or daughter of the King. You don't have to settle for lentils when God has prepared a feast for you.

When we understand what Jesus has done for us, it changes everything. Instead of living for the comforts of this world, we live with the eternal contentment that comes from knowing Heaven is our home. We learn to embrace discomfort today, knowing God is working all things for our good.

We stop making bad trades because we know the value of what we've received.

Esau traded his birthright for a bowl. Jesus, the firstborn Son, gave up His birthright to give it back to us. Now, the choice is ours. Will we cling to the fleeting comforts of this world, or will we embrace the lasting contentment of God's promises?

The table is set, and the feast is waiting. Come home and receive the birthright that is rightfully yours through Jesus. Don't settle for the bowl when the banquet is already prepared. Choose contentment over comfort and discover the joy of living in God's abundance.

CHALLENGE

COMFORT OR CONTENTMENT CHECK DAY

Place a checkmark next to the statement that best describes you currently—not who you aspire to be, but how you're living right now.

- ☐ You live past or up to the edge of your means.
- ☐ You live with financial margin (not spending more than you earn)
- ☐ You think having more will make you happy.
- ☐ You are happy with what you already have.
- ☐ You check your financial accounts more than you read God's Word.
- ☐ You read God's Word more than you check your financial accounts.
- ☐ You focus on short-term relief.
- ☐ You focus on long-term fulfillment.

#GIVINGCHALLENGE

☐	You see work as a way to accumulate for yourself.	☐	You see work as a way to serve others and glorify God.
☐	You want to outpace, or at least keep up, with your neighbors and friends.	☐	You celebrate the blessings of your neighbors and friends.
☐	You constantly compare yourself to others.	☐	You are grateful for what you have.
☐	You live with considerable financial debt.	☐	You live without considerable financial debt.
☐	You buy or get the things you want.	☐	You deny yourself some pleasures in this world.
☐	You avoid taking risks for fear of failure.	☐	You trust in God's plan, even when taking risks.
☐	You are consumed with what's next.	☐	You are content with where you are now.
☐	You avoid doing hard things.	☐	You do hard things.
☐	Your inner peace is tied to your outer circumstances.	☐	You have inner peace no matter your outer circumstances.

Count the number of checkmarks on the right side and circle the number below. If your number is low, you are likely prioritizing comfort. If your number is high, you are living with contentment.

Comfort 1 2 3 4 5 6 7 8 9 10 11 12 13 **Contentment**

Whatever your number might be, set a goal to improve by at least two or three points. What action or next steps can you take this week to get better? Write it down and act on it.

6/40

DAY 7

FROM RICHES TO RAGS BACK TO RICHES

> "I lay down my life—only to take it up again. No one takes it from me."
>
> John 10:17b-18a

Have you ever been comfortable but not content?

To be content is to be in a state of happiness and satisfaction. Contentment implies that you are at peace no matter what your circumstances may be.

Contentment is largely pursued with one of two strategies for Western Christians: Either you can find it in the grace of Jesus, or you can chase after it through the comfortable things of this world. To be fair, many attempt to find contentment through a combination of the two. During this week, you will be challenged to live not for the comfort that this world can provide but rather the contentment that Jesus offers to you.

As I invite you to trade the idea of pursuing worldly comfort for godly contentment, let's first see how this showed up in the life of Jesus.

If you believe in Jesus, you are abundantly rich because of God's grace. This is not just conjecture. These are the very words the apostle Paul laid out for us.

> **For you know the grace of our Lord Jesus Christ, that though he was rich, yet for your sake he became poor, so that you through his poverty might become rich. 2 Corinthians 8:9**

In this verse, not only does the apostle Paul claim that we are rich because of God's grace, but he reminds us that Jesus, who was rich, became poor for us.

Some say the greatest test, or proof, of your love is what you are willing to give up for someone else. And Jesus proved this test by giving up His very life for you and for me.

> **But God proves His love for us in this: While we were still sinners, Christ died for us. Romans 5:8 (BSB)**

Not only did Jesus rescue us when we were at our worst, but He did it, you could argue, when He was at His best. While we were still sinners, do you know where Jesus was? He was seated in power, in control, sovereign over all on His throne in full and complete glory.

Here's how Isaiah 6:1b-4 describes it:

> **I saw the Lord, high and exalted, seated on a throne; and the train of his robe filled the temple. Above him were seraphim, each with six wings: With two wings they covered their faces, with two they covered their feet, and with two they were flying. And they were calling to one another:**
>
> > **"Holy, holy, holy is the LORD Almighty;**
> > **the whole earth is full of his glory."**
>
> **At the sound of their voices the doorposts and thresholds shook and the temple was filled with smoke.**

God gave Isaiah this vision of the pre-incarnate Jesus in the throne room, seated on the throne, high and exalted. To be seated on a throne means the One seated is in control. He is sovereign and powerful. The massive train of His robe, symbolizing power, fills the entire Temple. Even before His victory over the devil, His robe is that majestic!

Around Him are angels with six wings, flying and worshiping, crying out, "Holy, Holy, Holy is the Lord Almighty." This triple repetition emphasizes God's perfect holiness. Gazing upon His glory, "holy" is the only word they can repeat, as they were overwhelmed by His presence.

As they worshiped, the doorposts and thresholds of the Temple shook, and the Temple was filled with smoke. These inanimate objects—things that have no breath to breathe, no eyes to see, or ears to hear—somehow joined in the worship of God at that moment. How amazing! In other sections of Scripture, we know that all creation, not just angels, but mountains, oceans, Sun, Moon, and stars, praises God, with lightning and thunder in the background displaying His glory.

This is where Jesus was, in Heaven, when He looked down and saw us sinning and acting like fools. Now ask yourself, would you leave that? When He was in Heaven, He was already ultimately rich, and He had all this glory. So, why would He get up off the throne?

THE MISSING PIECE

There was only one key piece missing from this eternal worship scene. You and me. To get us there, He knew His life was the required payment. He gave up everything of Himself for you and for me.

<u>God left the comfort of Heaven because He was not content being there without you.</u>

#GIVINGCHALLENGE

Pastor Timothy Keller says, "If He had not become poor, had He not been born in a manger, had not endured the cross, had not been emptied of His glory, He wouldn't have had us. He'd have stayed in Heaven, He'd kept His riches, and we would have been lost."[14]

In Jesus's own words, He reminds us that He was not forced into this.

> **"The reason my Father loves me is that I lay down my life—only to take it up again. No one takes it from me, but I lay it down of my own accord. I have authority to lay it down and authority to take it up again."**
> **John 10:17-18a**

He willingly and lovingly chose a path that would include a brutal death that He didn't deserve.

Do you know what that means? In some sense, we must be more precious to Him than the rest of the universe because He gave it all up. When we see Jesus going to the cross because He treasures us, you would think the only natural response, in return, would be to make Him our ultimate treasure.

If you have received nothing in this world, but you have received the grace of Jesus, you are rich. Period.

The grace of Jesus, poured out for you, is undeserved. It's unexpected. It's worth more than any amount of treasure you can accumulate in this world. Grace is the gift that allows you entrance into eternal life with Jesus. Grace is the gift that brings contentment to you and to me.

Content people learn how to be generous just like Jesus. We give because Jesus first gave to us. This world is not about seeking to maximize our personal comfort. It's about learning to grow with a heart like Jesus that says I will do whatever I need to do to help others receive God's grace. Even when I must sacrifice my own comforts of this world, I will do it because this is what Jesus has done for me.

Jesus treasured you so much that He gave His life for you.

Will you, in return, treasure Jesus above all else?

#GIVINGCHALLENGE

CHALLENGE

LOOK TO JESUS DAY

Answer the following questions as you reflect on how Jesus traded comfort for contentment:

Read 2 Corinthians 8:9 again. How does understanding Jesus's sacrifice of leaving the comforts of Heaven to become poor for your sake change your perspective on contentment?

_____

_____

Read Hebrews 12:1-3 and respond to this question: How do we know from the Bible that Jesus gave happily?

_____

_____

What specific part of Jesus's humanity is a comfort to you? That He knows what loneliness feels like? Maybe physical pain?

_____

_____

7/40

DAY 8

THE LIE OF MORE

"I have come that they may have life, and have it to the full."
John 10:10b

I remember the day I preached about materialism and totally missed the mark. My goal was to show how we fall for tactics that push us toward worldly comfort instead of godly contentment. Ironically, my message had the opposite effect.

It was the first Sunday of 2020, and for a sermon illustration, I brought out a massage gun I had just bought Allison for Christmas. At the time, massage guns were new and intriguing, so it got everyone's attention. I turned it on and preached for a minute using the massage gun on my chest. Of course, my voice reverberated, and it created a humorous moment.

Through the illustration, I aimed to show how marketing convinces us of problems we never knew existed, leading us to chase more while remaining unsatisfied. The massage gun didn't exist years ago, but once we had it, Allison and I couldn't imagine life without it.

However, instead of prompting repentance from materialism, my message led people to ask where they could buy a massage gun. Rather than pointing them to Jesus, I unintentionally fed their discontent. And, ironically, in a book about giving, you might even be tempted to get one for yourself right now. Resist that urge. That's the point of putting this example in the book—to show how we are easily swayed.

Effective marketing starts with this question: "What's in it for me?" They call this the WIIFM question. The best marketers will convince you of problems you didn't even know you had. They tell you how their product, their service, their subscription, their fill-in-the-blank will make your life even greater. It is said the average American sees between 4,000 and 10,000 ads per day.[15]

And we fall for them, hook, line, and sinker.

DIRECT AND INDIRECT ADS

Advertisers are good. They spend a ton of money, and they scream this so-called "truth" at you everywhere: The more you have, the happier you will be.

Sometimes it's super direct.

With the rise of artificial intelligence, targeted ads are getting better and better. I can mention a specific golf club out loud to friends or family that I think will transform my golf game (that's never worked for me, by the way), and then suddenly I'll start seeing ads for it pop up on random websites that have nothing to do with the product. When I lost my luggage recently, I started seeing luggage ads to replace my 20-year-old bag that I loved with the newest model.

Sometimes it's more indirect.

A news article highlighted how TV shows influence behavior. For example, after HBO's *White Lotus* featured Sicily, tourism searches for the location increased by 50 percent. Similarly, *Game of Thrones* boosted interest in Croatia, and *Yellowstone* spiked visits to U.S. National Parks.[16]

Why does this happen? What we see and hear shapes our desires. Before *White Lotus*, many wouldn't have considered Sicily, but stunning visuals spark thoughts like, "I need to go there to be happy." And, again, the thing you will have to fight right now is the urge to look up for yourself what a vacation in Sicily will look like.

I would argue that the world's "truth" that getting more will make you happy has already been exposed over and over as a lie, and yet we continue to fall for it. The more we fall for it, our comfort levels may rise, but we become more discontent.

In the Old Testament, a king named Solomon was the richest man in the world. He once said, **"Whoever loves money never has enough; whoever loves wealth is never satisfied with their income. This too is meaningless." Ecclesiastes 5:10.**

In the New Testament, the apostle Paul wrote these words to Timothy: **"But godliness with contentment is great gain. For we brought nothing into the world, and we can take nothing out of it." 1 Timothy 6:6-7**

What was true in both the Old and New Testament is also true for us today. If you continue to chase for more and more of this world, you'll never have enough.

There was once a man who owned 1 percent of the entire wealth of the U.S. economy. He puts guys today like Musk, Bezos, Gates, and Buffett to shame. He was the world's first billionaire. His name was John D. Rockefeller. One time, reportedly, someone asked him how much money is enough money. His answer: "Just a little bit more."

King Solomon, the apostle Paul, and John D. Rockefeller show us that if your pursuit is for more, you'll never have enough. If you are going to chase possessions, net worth, vacations, and anything else you can put your hands on, you may find comfort, but you will not be content.

The world teaches us a way of life that will eventually destroy you.

So, here's the option that Jesus offers: Everything you need you already have in Him. As Jesus once said, **"I have come that they may have life, and have it to the full." John 10:10b**

Jesus came to give you what you most needed. It has already been supplied by God to you in the life, death, and resurrection of Jesus. You don't need to live for more to be happier.

In other words, true lasting happiness is not found in a massage gun, a golf club, or a vacation to Sicily.

I want to be clear in this message. God is not saying it's bad to be rich or have possessions, but it is bad if the possessions become what you trust in or what you look to for happiness. Happiness is found when you receive the gift of grace that Jesus offers to you—a gift that leads not only to your eternal life, but to a life of contentment today. As you receive Jesus's gift and learn how to be generous like Him, a whole new world of joy and happiness awaits you.

If you aren't there yet, that's okay, keep reading. I promise that this journey will end well for you! You'll hear stories along the way, not only of Jesus, but of people today who have given up comfort for contentment and discovered the joy it brings.

CHALLENGE

TRACK YOUR MONEY DAY

Track your monthly spending on entertainment during the last month. Here are some sample categories:

- Subscriptions like Netflix, Disney+, Hulu, Spotify, etc.
- Tickets for movies or plays
- Concert tickets
- Music purchases (vinyl, digital downloads, etc.)
- Game tickets (football, basketball, etc.)
- Sports and Fitness (gym memberships, sports leagues, etc.)
- Video games (purchases, subscriptions, in-game purchases)

- Gaming platforms (Xbox Game Pass, PlayStation Network, etc.)
- Festivals, fairs, or carnivals
- Comedy shows or other live entertainment
- Dining out for fun rather than necessity
- Drinks or coffee with friends for leisure
- Weekend getaways
- E-books, audiobooks, or hard copies
- Supplies for crafts or hobbies (e.g., painting, knitting, golfing)
- Lessons (e.g., dance, pottery, photography, piano)
- Theme park tickets
- Zoo or aquarium passes
- Devices or tools specifically for entertainment (e.g., VR headsets, headphones)
- Any other entertainment-related spending not captured above

DATE	CATEGORY	DESCRIPTION	AMOUNT

#GIVINGCHALLENGE

1 What patterns do you notice in your entertainment spending?
- Are there categories where you consistently spend more than expected? Are there any surprises about where your money is going?

_____

_____

2 Does your entertainment spending align with your values and financial priorities?
- Looking at your tracked expenses, do you feel your spending reflects what truly brings you joy and fulfillment, or are there areas where you might want to adjust?

_____

_____

3 If you needed to reduce entertainment spending by 10 to 20 percent, where would you start?
- Are there any subscriptions, habits, or impulse purchases you could adjust without sacrificing meaningful enjoyment? How might you redirect that money toward generosity, savings, or other priorities?

_____

_____

DAY 9
THE COMPARISON TRAP

> "Look at the birds of the air . . . Are you not much more valuable than they?"
> **Matthew 6:26**

I had always dreamed of taking my boys to a Major League Baseball game. That dream finally came true while visiting their grandparents in Wisconsin when we scored tickets to see the Milwaukee Brewers. Determined to make it memorable, we started with a tailgate in the parking lot before heading into the stadium.

After a long walk, we settled into our seats and cheered the Brewers to a victory over the Padres. Later, I posted a few pictures on Facebook (yes, I still use Facebook), showcasing our smiling faces. To anyone looking at the photos, it seemed like the day had been perfect—a dream fulfilled.

But reality couldn't have been further from that. My boys, ages seven and four, couldn't sit still for more than a minute. They didn't understand the appeal of tailgating and made it clear they thought eating hot dogs in a parking lot was the dumbest thing ever. They complained nonstop about the long walk to the stadium, and by the second inning they were so restless we had to wander around to find distractions. We stumbled upon a few kid-friendly activities. The boys ran the 60-foot dash and threw a ball as fast as they could, but those distractions lasted all of seven minutes.

The only surefire way to keep them content was buying food. Thanks to Dippin' Dots, I managed to secure a few moments of peace, but the game dragged on (this was before the pitch clock), and my bribery budget stretched thin. Somehow, amidst the chaos, I managed to snap a couple of photos with grandpa and the boys looking happy. But the truth? The day fell far short of my expectations.

This experience serves as a reminder: What we see on social media often isn't the whole story. Nona Jones, in her book *Killing Comparison*, writes, "Social media is a never-ending scroll of highlight reels. When we consume those highlights without balancing them against reality, we begin to believe our life is lacking in comparison."[17] My smiling photos told one story, but the reality was far messier. Life isn't always picture-perfect, and we shouldn't measure our own experiences or lives against someone else's highlight reel.

Our world has grown larger than ever thanks to social media, constantly exposing us to the lives of those who seem to have more. You might feel perfectly content after a vacation to Branson, Missouri, until you scroll and see your friend just spent a week in Paris. The one in France, not Texas. Maybe you were overjoyed taking your daughter to a Disney movie until you saw your friend sharing photos of their entire family at Disneyland. Maybe you were thrilled with your golfing trip to Scottsdale, only to spot a post about your friend's golf adventure in Scotland. Or you might have had a blast in Tuscaloosa cheering on the Crimson Tide, until you see someone else enjoying two weeks in Tuscany's wine country.

IS IT OKAY TO COMPARE?

It is hard to be content when we are bombarded all day long with people who love to share their highlight reels. It's impossible for our real life to live up to someone else's highlight-reel life.

Unhealthy comparison always brings discontentment.

So, is comparison always something to avoid? Interestingly, Jesus addresses this human tendency to compare in Matthew 6:25-27:

> "Therefore I tell you, do not worry about your life, what you will eat or drink; or about your body, what you will wear. Is not life more than food, and the body more than clothes? Look at the birds of the air; they do not sow or reap or store away in barns, and yet your heavenly Father feeds them. Are you not much more valuable than they? Can any one of you by worrying add a single hour to your life?"

What stands out is that Jesus doesn't tell us to avoid comparison entirely. Instead, He invites us to a healthy comparison.

Healthy comparison brings contentment.

Rather than measuring ourselves against others, He says, "Look at the birds." If God provides for them, how much more will He care for us, His most valuable creation? This type of comparison can remove your worry and bring strong mental health.

Why? Because this kind of comparison reminds you of God's love and provision, grounding you in contentment.

Comparison, then, can be healthy or unhealthy. The danger, of course, is that I bet you haven't spent time thinking about or comparing yourself with birds lately. The measuring test is in your comparison. Are you feeling more or less content?

The more content you become in Jesus, the more you'll reflect His character. When you're spiritually healthy on the inside, you're far more effective in living out His mission. His love and provision not only bring contentment but also fuel you to become more like Him.

Comparison doesn't just impact our contentment; it can also shape how we view generosity. When we stop measuring ourselves against others and focus instead on God's provision, it frees us to give, not out of obligation or competition, but out of gratitude and love.

When it comes to generosity, we're often taught to avoid discussing our giving publicly. In many cases, that may be true. In Matthew 6, Jesus warns us not to be like the Pharisees who give solely for public recognition. If the goal of our generosity is self-promotion, or maybe a social media post with as many likes as possible, then that principle absolutely applies. But there are moments in Scripture where sharing about generosity isn't for the spotlight but to inspire others toward good works and the joy of giving.

Take King David, for example. He wanted to build a temple for God, but God revealed that this task would be fulfilled by his son Solomon. In response, David did something truly beautiful. He set up the next generation for success. Using his wisdom, position, and resources, David raised funds for the Temple. To encourage others, he publicly shared his intentions and his contribution: *This is what I'm giving. This is what the leaders are giving. Now, you should give too.* His purpose wasn't self-glorification but glorifying God.

In this book, you'll see Jesus, the Ultimate Giver, in action. You'll also encounter stories of astounding generosity, both in Scripture and in the lives of people today. These stories may inspire you to evaluate your own giving. Healthy comparison, though, isn't about condemnation but conviction. It might challenge you to do more, which is not necessarily a bad thing.

Each story will likely show the highlight reel of generosity. Occasionally, you'll glimpse the struggles or sacrifices behind it. But remember: We're all on a journey to become more like Christ.

Along that journey, it's incredible to know that no matter what we do, God will provide for us. We don't need to measure ourselves against someone else's highlight reel. Instead, we can compare ourselves to the birds of the air and see how deeply we are loved. That love fuels us to live generously, just as Jesus has done for you and for me.

PRAY DAY

Every week, you will be challenged to pray about your giving. As you discern what/how to give each week, you will never be told a specific amount. Our recommendation for you is to bring all these decisions before God through prayer.

Here are the prayer steps we'll be asking you to follow each week:

1 Acknowledge that God is most generous and thank Him for His provision.

2 Ask God how you can be generous this week.

3 Listen for His direction. For specifics on how to hear God's voice, check out this blog: "3 Questions to Help You Know if You Are Hearing God's Voice."

4 Be obedient. When God is leading you to give, follow His lead and trust Him fully.

#GIVINGCHALLENGE

Here's a model of a prayer we will ask you to pray each week:

Heavenly Father,

I come before You today with an open heart, asking You to guide me in my giving. You are the Ultimate Provider, and all I have comes from You. Lord, what would You have me give? I desire to give happily, to trade worldly comfort for godly contentment. So, God, please show me where and how I can be generous this week so I can reflect Your heart and truly make a difference in the lives of others.

God, I'm quieting my heart and listening for Your direction. Give me discernment to recognize Your voice now and clarity to follow where You lead.

Consider pausing in silence for a minute or two.

Lord, I choose to trust You. I will respond with obedience. I know that You see the bigger picture, that You have my best in mind, and that You will always provide for my needs. Help me to release any fear or hesitation, and to give with a joyful heart. May my giving be an act of worship that draws me closer to Your heart.

In Jesus's name,
Amen.

DAY 10

MONEY NUMBERS

> "Come to me, all you who are weary and burdened, and I will give you rest."
> **Matthew 11:28**

"Hey, what's your money number?"

That question was casually tossed out in my foursome as we stood on the tee box, waiting for the group ahead of us to finish their shots on a short par 3.

"What do you mean?" I asked.

"How much money would you need today to feel comfortable?" my friend continued. "To stop worrying about money and to not care what anyone else thinks?"

The other players tossed out their numbers. One said $50 million. Another $100 million.

Then it was my turn. I stammered, not sure how to answer. Finally, I mumbled something about how, in ministry, you just don't think like that, and I never gave a number. Thankfully, it was time to golf. I duck-hooked my 8-iron off the tee and missed the green. No one seemed to notice I'd dodged the question. But I couldn't stop thinking about it. What would my number be? Should I even have a number?

At first, I thought their numbers were outrageous. "I could be comfortable with way less than that," I told myself. But the more I thought about it, the more the question stuck with me. I set goals for so many areas of life: careers, relationships, fitness. So why not money? Should I have a "number"? And if I did, what would it say about what I value?

For most people, there's no clear endgame when it comes to money. Without one, we're left vulnerable to the endless pursuit of "more," with no guardrails to protect us. It's easy to get caught in the rat race, striving for a moving target we can never fully reach.

And if we don't define our financial goals, society is all too ready to step in with its own standards.

SOCIETY'S NUMBERS

In 2024, a study from SmartAsset determined the salary Americans needed to live "comfortably." For an individual, the magic number was $96,500. For a family of four, it was a staggering $235,000.

In Omaha, Nebraska, my hometown, the estimate was slightly lower: $223,891.[18]

When I read those numbers, I couldn't help but think, is this going to make people who don't measure up feel "less-than"? I have a family of four in Omaha, and we don't hit that number. Yet, we feel far more comfortable than most.

In fact, I know families living on half, or even a third or a quarter, of that amount who are happy, fulfilled, and generous. Which made me wonder: Are we aiming at the wrong targets?

The SmartAsset study broke things down using the 50/30/20 rule:

- 50 percent for necessities (housing, groceries, transportation)
- 30 percent for entertainment and hobbies
- 20 percent for savings, investments, or paying off debt

Notice what's missing? Generosity.

The one thing Jesus consistently taught, and modern research supports as a true pathway to joy, doesn't even factor into the formula.

This makes me think our obsession with comfort through wealth accumulation is flawed at its core.

Jesus offers us a better pursuit: not comfort, but contentment.

THE SECRET OF CONTENTMENT

Here's the thing about contentment: It doesn't have a number.

That doesn't mean numbers aren't important. It's wise to have budgets and financial plans. But contentment is a deeper reality that isn't tied to how much or how little you have.

Contentment can thrive in both abundance and lack. It's present when the bank account is full, and it can endure when resources are scarce.

The apostle Paul explained it like this in Philippians 4:11b-13:

> **I have learned to be content whatever the circumstances. I know what it is to be in need, and I know what it is to have plenty. I have learned the secret of being content in any and every situation, whether well fed or hungry, whether living in plenty or in want. I can do all this through him who gives me strength.**

Paul wrote these words from a prison cell—a far cry from worldly comfort. He had experienced success, influence, and wealth in his earlier life. But when Jesus called him, Paul left those pursuits in exchange for something far better: a life of purpose, significance, and lasting contentment in Christ.

Contentment isn't about ease or luxury. Jesus never promised us that. What He did promise was rest:

> **"Come to me, all you who are weary and burdened, and I will give you rest."** Matthew 11:28

This is the invitation: to step off the treadmill of chasing more and to walk with Jesus instead. In Him, we find a rest that's deeper than physical comfort. It's the kind of rest that brings peace to your soul, no matter what numbers define your bank account.

As I reflected on that moment on the tee box, I wasn't prepared to give a number. The truth is, I don't need one. Nor do you. True contentment isn't found in a salary figure or a bank statement. While it's wise to have financial goals in life, contentment is not tied to societal benchmarks or fleeting comforts. My contentment is in Christ alone, and that's more than enough.

As I've learned this week, the real question isn't "What's your money number?" It's this:

What are you chasing, and where is it leading you?

PREP DAY

Yesterday you prayed about a gift that you can give away. Tomorrow you will be encouraged to give your gift away.

Write down the gift you are feeling led to give tomorrow. You can write the amount and who you'd like to give the gift to. It can be a person, an organization, or your local church.

AMOUNT: _____

RECIPIENT: _____

As you write your potential gift down, pause and pray. In your prayer, ask God these three questions.

1. Is my gift generous?
2. Is my gift sacrificial?
3. Is my gift obedient?

#GIVINGCHALLENGE

- If the answers are "yes," then ask God to guide you in staying faithful to your decision.

- If the answers are "maybe," consider if God is asking you to give more.

- If the answers are "no," practice writing a higher number until you feel confident that what you are giving is generous, sacrificial, and obedient.

Let your giving reflect the contentment you have from Christ, knowing that He has, is, and will take good care of you each and every day.

10/40

DAY 11

COMFORT ZONE

> "But the Comforter, *even* the Holy Spirit, whom the Father will send in my name, he shall teach you all things, and bring to your remembrance all that I said unto you."
>
> **John 14:26 (ASV)**

In the fall of 2011, I felt a clear calling from God to help as many people as possible learn to follow Jesus. My mission was simple: point people directly to the life, words, and habits of Jesus. After all, if He is the One we're called to model our lives after, why not focus entirely on Him?

For six years, this mission progressed slowly. But in 2017, I felt it was time to go all in. That meant taking a significant financial leap to bring a vision to life, writing my first book, *Red Letter Challenge*. To make it happen, I partnered with an incredible design company to bring the project to fruition. It was exciting and uncharted territory for me. But to do it well required stepping far outside of our financial comfort zone.

We didn't have the money we needed. In fact, our family had already taken a significant financial hit the year before. After much prayer and discussion, we decided to sacrifice what little savings we had and even asked a couple of close friends for their financial help. By God's grace, they gave generously, believing in the mission alongside us.

With that step of faith, the book was born. There was no guarantee it would succeed. Financially, it felt risky. Our safety net was gone. But spiritually, it was a leap of trust, handing over control to God and believing this work could bless people and that ultimately He would provide.

And He did! In ways we never imagined, God showed up and worked through *Red Letter Challenge*. This one book would turn into even more books (like the one you are reading now), as well as kids books, a podcast, and so much more. Seven years later, it's humbling to see the lives impacted and the fruit that has come from stepping out in faith.

Looking back, I've learned a valuable lesson:

God's greatest work often begins when we step outside of our comfort zones.

When we stretch our faith, especially in areas like finances, we open ourselves to experiencing the Holy Spirit in powerful ways. For me, stepping beyond what felt safe, particularly financially, has deepened my reliance on God and allowed me to experience His provision and presence in ways I never imagined. And I'm not alone on this journey. Many others have taken similar leaps of faith, embracing contentment over personal comfort, and their stories continue to inspire me.

CHOOSING WHAT IS BETTER

One such story is that of Tom Hsieh and his wife, Bree.

Tom Hsieh, once a CEO and co-owner of a telecom consulting firm, made a bold choice with his wife, Bree, to move to Pomona, California, one of the poorest cities in LA County. Instead of living according to their means, they decided to live at or below the city's median household income (around $45,000 at the time), giving the rest of their earnings away. This wasn't just a financial decision; it was a way to fully immerse themselves in the lives of their neighbors.

When Tom's employer, EarthLink, went public, his stock options made him a multimillionaire overnight. Yet, he and Bree chose to maintain their modest lifestyle, giving up the comforts of this world by continuing to drive an old three-cylinder Geo Metro while joyfully giving most of their income to Kingdom work. For Tom, generosity brought far greater satisfaction and contentment to his life than any luxury could.

Their choice to live in the inner city created unexpected and meaningful ministry opportunities. One afternoon, while out for a walk, Tom and Bree were approached by two boys who asked if they could teach them about the Bible. The boys returned week after week, eventually bringing their friends along.

Tom observed that this level of openness to the Gospel was something he had never encountered while living in the suburbs. Additionally, the Hsiehs opened their home to a troubled young girl, and within just a few weeks, they witnessed her life change in remarkable ways.

When neighbors with young children lost their apartment, Tom and Bree didn't hesitate to take them in, despite the challenges of having so many people under one roof. It wasn't always easy, but even their daughter, Cadence, saw the beauty in it.

"It's hard," she admitted, "but your heart grows bigger, and it's worth it."

By finding contentment in what God had provided for them, and living out their faith through radical generosity, the Hsiehs have found something far more valuable than wealth—lives filled with love, joy, and eternal impact. In choosing simplicity and selflessness, they've discovered what it truly means to live richly.[19]

Their story reminds me how God often invites us to step beyond what feels safe or familiar. Whether it's giving sacrificially, opening our homes, or saying "yes" to an opportunity that challenges us, stepping out in faith creates space for God to move in powerful ways.

But let's be honest, stepping out isn't easy. It pushes us past our limits, forcing us to lean on God for strength and comfort. And that's exactly where the Holy Spirit meets us.

In our red-letter words for today, Jesus promises that the Holy Spirit is our comforter, teacher, and guide. The Spirit doesn't just help us remember what Jesus said; He empowers us to live it out, even when it feels uncomfortable. Often, it's in those moments of discomfort and stretching when we sense the Spirit's presence most clearly.

Many of us pray, "God, give me more of Your Spirit," but here's the truth: If you believe in Jesus, the Holy Spirit is already fully with you. What holds us back isn't a lack of the Spirit. It's our attachment to worldly comforts. When we cling to this world, our faith stagnates, and our need for the Spirit diminishes.

So, let me ask you: When was the last time you stepped far enough outside your comfort zone that you needed the Holy Spirit to sustain you? If your life looks no different than someone who doesn't know Jesus—waking up, working, eating, and settling in for a Netflix binge—how can you truly experience the Spirit's comfort?

Here's the thing: The Holy Spirit doesn't comfort us so we can stay comfortable. He comforts us when we step out in faith, take risks for God's kingdom, and live lives that depend on Him.

So, what's one bold step of faith God is asking you to take today?

When we leave the safety net of worldly comforts, we experience the extraordinary strength and peace of the Holy Spirit. And that's where true life begins.

So, take that step. Trust God. And watch as He moves in ways you never dreamed.

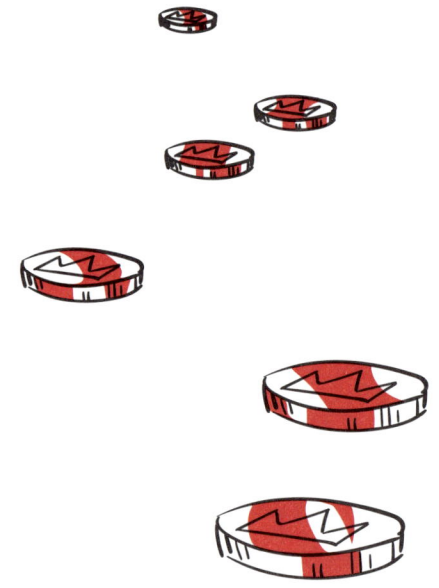

#GIVINGCHALLENGE

CHALLENGE

GIVE DAY

Today, you are being challenged to give your first of five gifts during these 40 days. Today's gift is meant to help you step out of your comfort zone.

All this week, you have studied how Jesus gave happily. You have looked at how much you spend on fun things like eating out, you swapped out some comfort, and you chose instead to be content. That trade should leave you with a little extra money to give away. Finally, you prayed about and prepared for what God wants you to do with the surplus.

If you feel led by God, give away some money today to someone who could use the contentment that God provides.

DAY 12

MARGIN AND ENOUGH

"Take my yoke upon you and learn from me, for I am gentle and humble in heart, and you will find rest for your souls."

Matthew 11:29

John Cortines, in his mid-20s, was earning a six-figure salary and aiming for early retirement by 40 as a diligent saver. Greg Baumer, earning over $250,000 annually, embraced a lifestyle of luxury with his family. Both lifelong Christians gave 10 percent of their income to the church, yet they felt unsatisfied. Could God be calling them to approach their finances differently?

The two men met at Harvard Business School and embarked on a massive generosity study that ended up transforming their lives. Their study resulted in writing one of my favorite modern-day books on generosity called *True Riches*.

In it, they summarize two keys to living with contentment: margin and enough.

MARGIN

What stops some of us from being generous financially is a real practical issue. We just don't feel like we have the money to do it. So, what do we do?

Cortines and Baumer write, "We consider margin to be the number-one principle for successful money management, because without it you cannot consistently give or save."[20] Margin is the difference between how much money you earn vs. how much money you spend.

Andy Stanley once said, "You should be knowing where your money is going." Creating margin often starts by creating a budget and then living by it and sticking to it. I know from experience that without a budget in place, it's easy for so much of my money to go to places that aren't really all that important to me or don't reflect my values.

Jesus created margin in His life. He had the most important mission of anyone who ever lived in this world. He had demands on His schedule constantly. And yet, despite everything going on around Him, Jesus always ensured that He spent quiet time with God. In fact, Luke 5:16 reminds us of this:

> **But Jesus often withdrew to lonely places and prayed.**

Rather than being bombarded by the world and doing what everyone else wanted or needed of Him, Jesus ensured that He was operating out of a healthy relationship with God.

Just as Jesus created margin with His time, we must do the same with our money. Without it, the world's demands will overwhelm us, making its agenda feel urgent. Instead, Jesus invites us to step away and spend time with Him. In Matthew 11:29, He says, **"Take my yoke upon you and learn from me, for I am gentle and humble in heart, and you will find rest for your souls."**

The "yoke," mentioned over 60 times in the Bible, refers to a wooden beam linking two animals so they can work together effectively. As followers of Jesus, our goal is to be "yoked" with Him. When we are, we can accomplish more than we ever could alone while maintaining a healthy relationship with God. Just as we must manage our time, we must manage our finances according to God's desires.

Scripture never calls us to live financially maxed out. If you're spending all you earn, or even more than you earn, you can't truly live generously. While the idea of spending less may feel uncomfortable, creating margin, even with lifestyle changes, is essential to finding contentment and becoming the generous person God calls you to be.

ENOUGH

On the other end of the spectrum, what may stop those with a high income from truly being generous is never defining what "enough" looks like. If you don't define "enough," then the world will tell you to just keep chasing. The problem with this pursuit is you'll never get to the finish line, and, therefore, you will never be satisfied.

I've written before about Thomas Aquinas, an Italian theologian who lived in the 13th century. Once, he was asked what would satisfy our desire to be happy. In other words, what would it take for a human to feel satisfied? Here is his answer:

> "Everything. We would have to experience everything and everybody and be experienced by everything and everybody to feel satisfied. Eat at every restaurant; travel to every country, every city, every exotic locale, experience every natural wonder; make love to every partner we could possibly desire; win every award, climb to the top of every field; own every item in the world; etc. We would have to experience it all to ever feel satisfied."[21]

Clearly, there has to be a better way. Rather than pursuing maximum comfort by experiencing all the things of this world, Jesus invites us to walk with Him and to live generously. When you are truly generous, you will find more satisfaction than you ever thought possible.

So, what's your "enough" finish line? Do you have one?

If you don't have a financial finish line or something you're aiming for, it's easy to fall into the trap of thinking that you're living generously if you just give a certain percentage. This is the mindset that Cortines and Baumer realized they were stuck in. They argue that to maximize our generosity and impact, we must shift the question from, "How much do I need to give?" to, "How much do I really need to keep?" This is what they call their finish line number.

FINISH LINE

Cortines and Baumer didn't just embrace this question; they are living it out. Both were so profoundly impacted by Jesus's teachings on money that they gave up their successful careers to pursue roles in which they could help others grow in generosity. They realized that mindlessly giving a percentage of their income to the church didn't necessarily make them feel generous or fulfilled.

After completing their study, they set their annual spending finish line at $100,000, regardless of how much they earned. While that number may seem high to some, what's remarkable is that they have one. For them, any income beyond that figure goes directly into God's Kingdom.

Their finish line allows for a comfortable lifestyle while providing guardrails to prevent living in excess. Your number may differ, but establishing a finish line is key to living contentedly with what God has given so you can practice true generosity.

As the Cortines family's income grew, they kept their finish line intact. In 2017, their first year of this new approach, they aimed to give $20,000 but ended up giving $36,494, representing 23 percent of their income.[22] They turned down buying a new car, choosing contentment instead. Each year, as God blesses them financially, their giving amount and percentage continue to grow. The same is true of the Baumer family.

Setting a finish line and giving more to God's Kingdom has brought them far greater satisfaction than their previous way of living ever could.

Pursuing worldly comfort endlessly will only leave you drained. True rest for your soul comes from finding contentment in what God has provided. This contentment not only brings peace to your life but also frees you to live generously. That choice blesses both you and others.

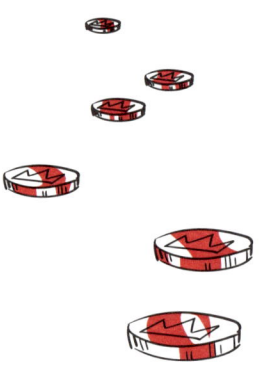

CHALLENGE

WRAP-UP DAY

Today, as we wrap up the Giving Happily week, I pray you feel a little more content, or a little happier inside. Spend some time reflecting on your gift and how you can keep trading comfort for contentment in your life.

If you gave yesterday, how did it feel?

_____

_____

_____

What would it look like to permanently trade comfort for contentment in your life?

_____

_____

_____

What was one major takeaway, feeling, or lesson that you received from this week's devotions and challenges?

_____

_____

_____

12/40

DAYS 13-19

OF THE 40-DAY CHALLENGE

WEEK 3: GIVING ETER

TRADING OWNERSHIP FOR STEWARDSHIP

"Life does not consist in an abundance of possessions."

Luke 12:15b

DAY 13

MAKING HOTELS INTO HOMES

> "But seek first his kingdom and his righteousness, and all these things will be given to you as well."
> Matthew 6:33

I had an incredible opportunity to travel and share the Gospel with thousands of teenagers. It was the kind of moment I'd dreamed of, so I wanted to be at my best.

I arrived a couple of days early to avoid flight delays or bad weather. The hotel was decent, but immediately I noticed some issues. Have you ever used those tiny, scratchy hotel towels? That's what I was dealing with. And the pillows? Not even close to my three-pillow-at-home setup: one under my head, one between my knees, and one to hug. I opened the blinds and spotted a Wal-Mart next door. It felt like a sign from God Himself.

At Wal-Mart, I picked up a soft, oversized towel (on rollback, thank you very much) and a Tempur-Pedic-style pillow. Since I happened to be in the bedding section, I noticed some sheets that had a nice thread count. I also remembered some of those "black light specials" on Dateline and thought I never can be too careful about hotel sanitation. I didn't want anybody else's germs ruining my big moment, so I threw a set of sheets into my cart.

As I brought my cart to the front, I remembered there was a wall air-conditioning unit in my hotel room. The last hotel I was at had this same unit and made a really weird, loud, clicking noise that made it hard to sleep. At that moment, I realized there was no way I should sacrifice my sleep here. Out of the corner of my eye, I noticed this sweet Dyson bladeless fan. It was quite a bit of money, but I needed to be fresh. So, I threw it into the cart.

As I went to checkout, in my peripheral vision, I saw they had a monster sale on TVs. My hotel room only had a 32-inch TV, and I'm not even sure it offered HD. My TV at home is 65 inches and in 4K, and I didn't want to miss the big game while I was on the road. So, because the sale was so great, I piled this new 65-inch TV into my cart.

I checked out and started driving back when I saw this new, big, state-of-the-art outdoor mall. I didn't think I needed anything else, but I had a couple of hours left to kill.

So, before I went back with all of my new stuff, I thought there's no harm in looking, right?

One of the first stores I came to had new exercise equipment. Before I go on stage, I like to spend some time exercising with my headphones on while worshiping God. I remembered that the exercise equipment they had in the hotel fitness center wasn't up to my liking. Not many hotels invest in their fitness equipment. Because of the enormity of the conference, I needed to be at my best, so I went into this store. I'd always heard of Peloton bikes but never had a chance to try one. The salesman encouraged me to give it a shot, so I hopped on it and was immediately sold. After a test ride, I arranged for the free setup and delivery straight to my room.

Then, right before I checked out from the store, I noticed the massage gun section. I had bought Allison a massage gun the past Christmas, and it had also done wonders for me. Anytime a muscle is sore, or a little achy, this thing would work for a couple of minutes, and I'd feel like a new man.

I had thought about bringing the one from home with me, but I didn't want to bring anything called a "GUN" through airport security, so I left it at home. It felt like a bit much, but I'd stayed in hotel rooms prior and sometimes woke up more sore or achy than in my home environment. So, I decided it'd be a good investment to purchase this as well.

Finally, after grabbing some dinner, I went back to the hotel room. All worked out really well. I watched the big game in glorious HD, cooled by my Dyson fan, and slept like a king under fresh Egyptian thread count sheets with my new Tempur-Pedic pillow. The next morning, I cycled on my Peloton, showered with my oversized towel, and worked out the kinks with my massage gun, arriving at the conference feeling 100 percent. I then delivered one of the most faith-filled, God-inspired, life-changing messages of my life.

INVEST IN WHAT LASTS

Hopefully, at some point in this really long and ridiculously fictitious parable, you realized it is a completely fabricated story. I'm not sure at what point you might have caught on, but before you did, hopefully you were thinking, "Zach, you are crazy! Why would you invest so much money into your hotel room, which is not your home? Zach, why would you spend so much money on stuff for only two nights, which are just a blip on the radar of your entire life—stuff that you can't take with you?"

Well, I want to ask you the same things. Why in the world would you spend so much money on stuff that, relative to eternity, is a blip on your radar? How many of you are filling your life with stuff that you will not be able to take with you?

This life is but a breath, a vapor, and then it's gone. The psalmist reminds us of this in Psalm 39:5: **"You have made my days a mere handbreadth; the span of my years is as nothing before you. Everyone is but a breath, even those who seem secure."**

#GIVINGCHALLENGE

Jesus came to remind us of this truth. In fact, if you look seriously at the words of Jesus, you will find that more than anything else, Jesus talked about the Kingdom of Heaven. As tempting as this world may be, Jesus encourages us over and over to seek and bring His Kingdom to this world. When we do, we'll have everything we need.

Jesus reminds us of this truth: **"But seek first his kingdom and his righteousness, and all these things will be given to you as well." Matthew 6:33**

As great as this life can be, as secure as you can try to make yourself in this world, rather than spending yourself for the sake of building your kingdom now, it's wiser to invest in the Kingdom of Heaven instead. For those who believe in the message of Jesus, the Kingdom of Heaven is your home, and your current life is like a two-night hotel stop. So, stop trying to turn a hotel into your home.

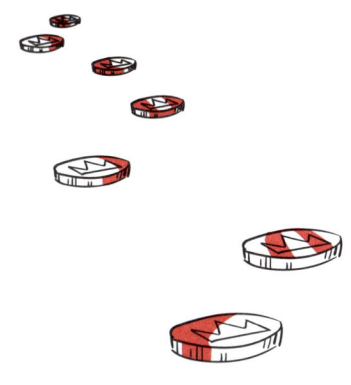

CHALLENGE

OWNER OR STEWARD CHECK

Place a checkmark next to the statement that best describes you currently—not who you aspire to be, but how you're living right now.

- ☐ You see all that you have as yours to control and protect.
- ☐ You feel entitled to what you've worked for.
- ☐ You see giving as losing what belongs to you.
- ☐ You take credit for your success.
- ☐ You save more money than you give.
- ☐ You feel responsible for holding onto everything tightly.
- ☐ You live trying to get the most out of life right now.
- ☐ You think more about retirement than you do heavenly rewards.
- ☐ You work to achieve personal recognition.

- ☐ You see all that you have as entrusted to you by God.
- ☐ You feel gratitude for what you've been given.
- ☐ You see giving as an opportunity to bless others.
- ☐ You credit God for your successes and opportunities.
- ☐ You give more money than you save.
- ☐ You trust that God will provide everything you need.
- ☐ You live with a focus on helping the next generations.
- ☐ You think more about heavenly rewards than you do retirement.
- ☐ You work to glorify God and serve others.

#GIVINGCHALLENGE

☐ You don't think about Heaven often.	☐ You think of Heaven often.
☐ You have no guidelines, limits, and normal budgeting practices.	☐ You have many guidelines, limits, and normal budgeting practices.
☐ You don't think about your financial decisions much.	☐ You view every financial decision in light of eternity.
☐ You have so much stuff that you're not sure what to do with it all.	☐ All your stuff has a purpose, and it's not overwhelming to think about.

Count the number of checkmarks on the right side and circle the number below. If your number is low, you are likely living with an Owner Mindset. If your number is high, you're embracing a Steward Mindset.

Owner 1 2 3 4 5 6 7 8 9 10 11 12 13 **Steward**

Whatever your number might be, set a goal to improve by at least two or three points. What action or next steps can you take this week to get better? Write it down and act on it.

DAY 14

THE ETERNAL GIFT OF GOD

> "For God so loved the world, that he gave his only Son, that whoever believes in him should not perish but have eternal life."
>
> **John 3:16 (ESV)**

What's the greatest proof that you love someone?

Search online, and you'll find answers like being present, showing support, keeping promises, forgiving, and being loyal. All of these are meaningful ways to express love. But the ultimate proof of love is what you're willing to do, endure, sacrifice, and give unconditionally for someone.

In the most famous Bible verse of all time, God's love is on display through a gift: His Son. John 3:16 (ESV) says, **"For God so loved the world, that he gave his only Son, that whoever believes in him should not perish but have eternal life."**

Love isn't proven by words or feelings but by actions. God the Father showed His love by giving us Jesus. Jesus demonstrated His love by giving His life for us on the cross. Giving is the ultimate test of love. If that's true, then God must really love you and me!

And why did He give? So that whoever believes in Him would not perish but have eternal life. Jesus didn't come to guarantee us wealth, comfort, or worldly blessings right now. His gift was given to us to secure a hope-filled eternity with Him.

The challenge we face between now and Christ's return is resisting the temptation to forget the promise of eternal life and instead live only for the moment. Tragically, countless people have been completely drawn in by this deception.

In a nation where over 63 percent of people still identify as Christian, social scientist Ryan Burge says only 33 percent of Americans believe strongly in an afterlife. The statistics are even more startling in Europe: Just 12 percent of people in France, Germany, and the Netherlands share a strong belief in an afterlife, and Italy ranks lowest at only 4 percent.[23]

When we get this wrong, we live with an entirely backwards perspective.

One example of how we've lost sight of this eternal reality is the rise of #YOLO. We're constantly bombarded with messages urging us to focus on the here and now, summed up in the popular phrase "You Only Live Once." While this motto could encourage us to make the most of our lives, it's often used to justify reckless or self-centered choices. It reflects a mindset that prioritizes immediate gratification over lasting purpose.

If this world is all there is and there is no afterlife, it would make complete sense to maximize every day that you can in this world. But if we truly believe in the eternal life Jesus offers, our perspective must shift. Life isn't limited to this moment; it extends beyond the grave into eternity. This reality challenges us to live not for ourselves, but for God's Kingdom and the purpose He's given us.

If you look into the words of Jesus, the proper theological understanding for believers is "You Actually Live Twice," or #YALT. You are living right now for a blip of time, but you will rise again at the resurrection of Jesus and live a second time, in eternity, with God. Running throughout His words, Jesus makes the case that those who live and think as if what we are experiencing now is all we have are foolish. We are only here for a short period of time.

#YALT

YOU ACTUALLY LIVE TWICE

#GIVINGCHALLENGE

LIAR, LUNATIC, OR LORD?

I'm not entirely sure how the math adds up here. I struggle to understand how someone can claim to believe in Jesus but not in the afterlife. To me, this points to a shallow or underdeveloped faith that seems to be spreading not only across America but around the world.

My instinct tells me that more and more people want to associate with Jesus in part, but they hesitate to look at His teachings. When we take this approach, we end up with a watered-down, lukewarm understanding of Jesus that does little to reflect who He truly is in a world that so desperately needs Him.

In *Mere Christianity*, C.S. Lewis addressed skeptics by presenting apologetic arguments about Jesus's identity. Lewis famously made the case that Jesus was either a liar, lunatic, or Lord.

Here's the quote in full context from his book:

> "I am trying here to prevent anyone saying the really foolish thing that people often say about Him: 'I'm ready to accept Jesus as a great moral teacher, but I don't accept His claim to be God.' That is the one thing we must not say. A man who was merely a man and said the sort of things Jesus said would not be a great moral teacher. He would either be a lunatic—on the level with the man who says he is a poached egg—or else he would be the Devil of Hell. You must make your choice. Either this man was, and is, the Son of God, or else a madman or something worse. You can shut Him up for a fool, you can spit at Him and kill Him as a demon; or you can fall at His feet and call Him Lord and God. But let us not come with any patronizing nonsense about His being a great human teacher. He has not left that open to us. He did not intend to . . . Now it seems to me obvious that He was neither a lunatic nor a fiend: and consequently, however strange or terrifying or unlikely it may seem, I have to accept the view that He was and is God."[24]

What I appreciate about the "liar, lunatic, or Lord" argument is that it forces us to make a choice. There's no room for a half-hearted, shallow belief in Jesus. As I look at how many express their faith today, I can't help but wonder if the enemy's most effective strategy right now is creating lukewarm believers. It's time to stop sitting on the fence and decide who Jesus really is for you: Is He a liar, a lunatic, or your Lord?

I'm not writing in this way to condemn anyone, but rather, to invite you to honestly consider the implications of your faith and who Jesus really is to you.

If He is a liar or a lunatic, then Jesus has no right to speak into how you live your life, and especially, for our purposes in this book, how you use your finances. You should stop reading this book and do what you want with your money.

But, if He is your Lord, that means you trust every promise He ever made, including that He is coming back to set up His Kingdom fully and you are a part of it! If there really is an afterlife—an eternal life—that impacts how you live today and how you use your resources. You begin to see this world differently, and you know that you were put here on this earth for a short period of time for a specific purpose. We'll dive much more deeply into that purpose in the coming days.

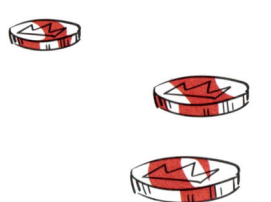

CHALLENGE

LOOK TO JESUS

To see Jesus in action as He chooses His eternal purpose over living for today, read Matthew 4:1-11. Write down how Jesus responded when Satan brought temptations to Him.

_____

_____

_____

How does understanding Jesus's sacrifice in John 3:16, where He paid for your sins to give you eternal life, shape the way you live your daily life?

_____

_____

_____

If someone observed your life, would they say you are living with eternity in mind or focused on the things of this world?

_____

_____

_____

14/40

DAY 15

OWNERS VS. STEWARDS

> "Well done, good and faithful servant!"
> Matthew 25:21a

We are bombarded all day long with messages that highlight YOU.

- YOU do YOU.
- Live YOUR truth.
- Follow YOUR heart.
- YOU deserve it.
- YOU only live once.

All of them make YOU the center of YOUR own universe. But YOU are not the center of the universe. YOU don't own anything. God owns it all.

All throughout the Bible, we see this truth played out. Let me show you a few places.

The whole earth is mine... Exodus 19:5b

To the LORD your God belong the heavens, even the highest heavens, the earth and everything in it. Deuteronomy 10:14

Everything under heaven belongs to me. Job 41:11b

If everything belongs to God, you know what else that means? You belong to God, too. A quick glance into the Bible, from front to back, reveals that God, in fact, owns you as well.

> **For you are a people holy to the LORD your God. The LORD your God has chosen you out of all the peoples on the face of the earth to be his people, his treasured possession. Deuteronomy 7:6**
>
> **But you are a chosen people, a royal priesthood, a holy nation, God's special possession, that you may declare the praises of him who called you out of darkness into his wonderful light. 1 Peter 2:9**
>
> **[Jesus Christ] gave himself for us to redeem us from all wickedness and to purify for himself a people that are his very own, eager to do what is good. Titus 2:14**

God owns you.

And, if you need just one more verse as evidence, how about 1 Corinthians 6:19b-20a?

> **You are not your own; you were bought at a price.**

Whoever pays for something becomes the owner. Jesus bought you with His blood at the cross. In a world that likes to make you think you are the center, you are not. You don't own you. God didn't put you in this world to be an owner; He put you here to be a steward.

FUNERAL WORDS

I once listened to a pastor share what he hoped people would say about him at his funeral. Naturally, it was what you'd expect. He hoped they expressed how much he loved and cared for Jesus, his family, and his close friends. He wanted to be remembered as someone who was faithful all the way to the end. But then he said something that struck me.

He explained that there was one thing he didn't expect anyone to say out loud, yet he hoped they would feel it deeply when reflecting on his life. He said, *"At the end of the day, I want people to think, 'He was a really good steward.'"*[25]

That simple yet profound statement has stayed with me. It's a reminder that true stewardship often speaks louder through actions than words, leaving an impact that's felt rather than declared.

God has placed each of us here to be stewards of what He has entrusted to us, and He gives to each person uniquely. A noble life is defined by how well we manage what God has given us, whether little or much. This truth is illustrated powerfully in the Parable of the Bags of Gold in Matthew 25:14-30.

The parable tells the story of a master who entrusts his wealth to three servants before leaving on a journey. Each servant receives an amount based on their ability: five bags of gold, two bags, and one bag. The first two servants immediately put the money to work, doubling what they were given. But the third servant, out of fear, hides his bag of gold in the ground, doing nothing with it.

When the master returns, he praises the first two servants for their faithfulness, rewarding them with greater responsibility and inviting them to share in his joy. However, he rebukes the third servant for his laziness and lack of trust, calling him wicked and casting him out.

The message of this parable is clear: God has entrusted each of us with resources and expects us to use them faithfully for His Kingdom. It's not about how much we've been given but about how we steward what God gives to us. When we know the master is returning, as in this parable, it's important we steward our resources today, not later, so that when the master returns, we've done everything we possibly can.

GOD OWNS OUR BUSINESS

Alan Barnhart and his brother took over the Barnhart Crane Rigging business from their father at a young age. Alan and his wife, Katherine, had always had a strong belief in God. Early on in the business, Alan read through everything the Bible said about money, and he came away with two major takeaways.

First, he was introduced to the concept of ownership vs. stewardship. An owner says, "It belongs to me," while a steward says, "It belongs to God." So, if everything I have comes from God and belongs to Him, then I need to be the best steward of His stuff that I can possibly be.

Second, he discovered that the Bible warned against greed resulting from business success. Greed isn't inevitable, for sure, but dozens of verses brought him to the conclusion that he needed to be careful to guard himself from the constant never-ending pursuit of more. He'd also seen evidence of this in others' lives. He didn't want greed to get the better of him.

So, Alan and Katherine made two decisions early on. On the business side, they decided that God in fact owns their business. Legally, they couldn't give away 100 percent of the business, so they gave away 99 percent to the National Christian Foundation (NCF), retaining only 1 percent in a trust. Although they still run the day-to-day business operations, they don't consider themselves owners of it, but stewards.

On the family side, they determined a "finish line" number for their income. This is a number that they were content to live on no matter what happened in their business. In the early days, this number was set at $40,000 and rose as high as $160,000 when they were taking care of their six kids. Alan is quick to admit that they aren't living a Mother Teresa lifestyle.

In the first year of making this change, Alan and his business gave away $50,000 to charity, more than Alan's salary. The business has exploded and grown from 10 employees to over 1,000. Revenue has gone from $1.5 million per year to over $400 million. Every year, they use half of their profit to grow their business and half to fund ministry. Altogether, they've been able to give more than $100 million for Kingdom purposes, and that number is escalating quickly.

When they look back on these decisions from decades ago, it's easy to see they wouldn't trade it for the world. They have found more joy in stewardship than ownership. Their net worth could be astronomical, but rather than chasing consumption and storing up stuff in as many barns as possible, the Barnharts have reflected the heart of God through their generosity and impacted countless lives across the world.

Although their last name is Barnhart, they've shown their heart is in anything other than bigger barns. I'm confident they will hear the words of Jesus that two of the three servants heard in the parable: **"Well done, good and faithful servant."** The question is, "Will you?"

#GIVINGCHALLENGE

CHALLENGE

TRACK YOUR MONEY

Last week, you tracked your entertainment. Now, if you have not done so already, track all your spending for the last month. This will help you create a budget. By looking at this monthly plan, you will not only know where your money is going, but you can set long-term financial goals, which will likely increase your opportunities to be generous.

Using the categories below, create a chart like the example below to track your spending in the last month. You can do this digitally using Microsoft Excel or Google Sheets, or with pen/paper. No matter your method, the goal is for you to understand where your overall expenses are going each month.

EXAMPLE:

GIVING	average per month	SAVINGS	average per month
Church	$30	Life Insurance	$50
Charity	$15	Stock Investments	$100
Gifts	$45	Retirement	$500
Other	$10	College Savings	$250
TOTAL GIVING	**$100**	**TOTAL SAVINGS**	**$900**

GIVING
Church
Charity
Gifts
Other
TOTAL

SAVINGS
Life Insurance
Stock Investments
Retirement
College Savings
TOTAL

HOME
Mortgage/Rent
Insurance
Repairs
Homeowner's Association
Utilities
Property Taxes
Other
TOTAL

15/40

GIVING ETERNALLY

DAILY LIVING
Groceries
Childcare
Entertainment
Eating Out
Other
TOTAL

TRANSPOR-TATION
Auto Loan
Insurance
Gas/Fuel
Maintenance
Other
TOTAL

MONTHLY BILLS
Cell Phone
Television
Internet
Apps/Streaming
Other
TOTAL

HEALTH
Insurance
Fitness
Prescriptions
Other
TOTAL

PERSONAL
Clothing
Hobbies
Books
Movies/Music
Other
TOTAL

MISCELLANEOUS
Education
Travel
Taxes
Pet
Other
TOTAL

1 What surprised you the most about your spending habits?

- Were there categories where you spent more than expected? Less than expected? Are there any areas where you can cut back to align better with your financial goals?

_____

_____

_____

#GIVINGCHALLENGE

2 **What steps can you take to be more intentional with your finances?**

- Are there specific categories where you could redirect funds toward savings, giving, or paying down debt? How can you make budgeting a regular habit to ensure long-term financial health and generosity?

_____

_____

_____

3 **If someone looked at all your spending, would they be able to discern that you are a follower of Jesus?**

- If yes, how could they tell? If no or maybe, how could your regular spending habits be altered to make this a reality?

_____

_____

_____

DAY 16
THE UNJUST STEWARD

> "For the sons of this world are more shrewd in dealing with their generation than the sons of light."
> **Luke 16:8b (NKJV)**

It has been labeled "The Most Difficult Parable to Understand."

In Luke, Jesus tells the parable known as "The Shrewd Manager" or "The Unjust Steward." The reason it is so difficult for us to comprehend is because it seems like Jesus makes the crook in this story the hero.

So, is that what's going on, or is there something more behind it? Let's find out.

He also said to His disciples: "There was a certain rich man who had a steward, and an accusation was brought to him that this man was wasting his goods. So he called him and said to him, 'What is this I hear about you? Give an account of your stewardship, for you can no longer be steward.'

"Then the steward said within himself, 'What shall I do? For my master is taking the stewardship away from me. I cannot dig; I am ashamed to beg. I have resolved what to do, that when I am put out of the stewardship, they may receive me into their houses.'" **Luke 16:1-4 (NKJV)**

In Jewish culture, it was common for wealthy individuals to employ stewards to manage their property and assets. In this parable, the steward had done a poor job and was about to be fired. Facing the reality of losing his job, he refused to resort to digging ditches or begging. Instead, he devised a sneaky plan to secure his future by going behind his master's back and renegotiating debts. While the parable mentions two such deals, it's likely he struck similar arrangements with others.

> "So he called every one of his master's debtors to *him*, and said to the first, 'How much do you owe my master?' And he said, 'A hundred measures of oil.' So he said to him, 'Take your bill, and sit down quickly and write fifty.' Then he said to another, 'And how much do you owe?' So he said, 'A hundred measures of wheat.' And he said to him, 'Take your bill, and write eighty.'" **Luke 16:5-7 (NKJV)**

By reducing the debts owed, the steward gained favor and secured friends so that when he was in a time of need, they would have his back. His actions were unjust, corrupt, wrong, and unfair to the master. Naturally, you'd expect the master to return and tear him to pieces. Yet, the response was surprisingly different.

> "So the master commended the unjust steward because he had dealt shrewdly." **Luke 16:8a (NKJV)**

The master didn't praise the steward for his dishonesty or corruption but for his shrewdness. To be shrewd is to be clever and astute and to demonstrate sharp judgment. While the steward's actions didn't benefit the master, the master had to admit the steward's resourcefulness.

PARABLES OF CONTRAST

If we stopped here, it would seem that Jesus is commending the man for being conniving, dishonest, and a crook. Is that what He wants from us as well? As long as we are shrewd, then we can let everything else go?

Of course not. So, before we dive into the end of the story, let's look at how Jesus taught. One third of the words of Jesus are parables—His primary way of teaching. Parables are stories designed to make a larger point, and with Jesus, the focus was always spiritual.

There are two main types of parables: comparison and contrast. Comparisons highlight similarities, while contrasts focus on differences. Luke, more than any other Gospel writer, often uses parables of contrast. Here, Jesus uses contrast to make His point. The steward in today's parable isn't a hero; he's a character meant to contrast a deeper truth about how we can better understand God and live faithfully.

HOW MUCH MORE?

Now, let's enter back into the story to see Jesus's response at the end of this parable to get the main point.

> **"For the sons of this world are more shrewd in their generation than the sons of light. And I say to you, make friends for yourselves by unrighteous mammon, that when you fail, they may receive you into an everlasting home." Luke 16:8b-9 (NKJV)**

Jesus isn't trying to convince us to be crooks or to be shrewd at all costs. By no means. He uses the unjust steward to show how much unbelievers often pursue their future with more passion, devotion, and focus than believers.

If an unjust steward would go to such lengths to plan for his future, how much more should we, as believers, invest in God's Kingdom? Sinful people will do almost anything to set themselves up for their future, but are we who believe using every means at our disposal to set up God's Kingdom now? Are we living like Heaven is our true home, using every opportunity to further God's plans without compromising who we are?

We aren't saved by works but by grace through faith. Yet, because of God's grace and the eternity awaiting us, we should never let unbelievers outdo us in preparing for a greater future. That includes how we handle money. Jesus uses money, or mammon, as an example here. He challenges us to think of our resources from an eternal perspective, recognizing that one day, our money will be gone, and our future will be realized. So, we may as well use our dollars for eternal purposes and invest it into the future that awaits all those who believe in Jesus Christ.

We are all stewards. The lesson isn't to be unjust, but to use what we have now wisely for eternal purposes. This parable highlights money but points to the larger truth that was Jesus's primary message: The Kingdom of Heaven is real, and it's coming. This life is short, and what we do with our time and resources truly matters.

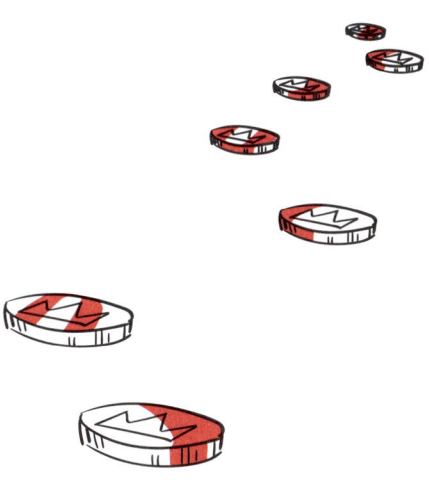

PRAY DAY

Every week you will be challenged to pray about your giving. As you discern what/how to give each week, you will never be told a specific amount. Our recommendation for you is to bring all these decisions before God through prayer.

Here are the prayer steps we'll be asking you to follow each week:

1 Acknowledge that God is most generous and thank Him for His provision.

2 Ask God how you can be generous this week.

3 Listen for His direction. For specifics on how to hear God's voice, check out this blog: "3 Questions to Help You Know if You Are Hearing God's Voice."

4 Be obedient. When God is leading you to give, follow His lead and trust Him fully.

#GIVINGCHALLENGE

If you need more direction, here's a prayer you can pray this week:

Heavenly Father,

I come before You today with an open heart, asking You to guide me in my giving. You are the Ultimate Provider, and all I have comes from You. Lord, what would You have me give? I desire to give a gift that will make an eternal difference in the lives of others. I pray that my generosity this week would reflect that You are the owner of all things, and I simply desire to be the best steward that I can possibly be.

God, I'm quieting my heart and listening for Your direction. Give me discernment to recognize Your voice now and clarity to follow where You lead.

Consider pausing in silence for a minute or two.

Lord, I choose to trust You. I will respond with obedience. I know that You see the bigger picture, that You have my best in mind, and that You will always provide for my needs. Help me to release any fear or hesitation, and to give with a joyful heart. May my giving be an act of worship that draws me closer to Your heart.

In Jesus's name,
Amen.

DAY 17

THE END IS COMING

> "Very truly I tell you, whoever hears my word and believes him who sent me has eternal life and will not be judged but has crossed over from death to life."
>
> John 5:24

Few phrases carry the weight of two words.

As you read through the following scenarios, think about what those words might be:

- You arrived just minutes after your plane took off.
- You turned in your assignment a day after it was due.
- You missed a milestone in your child's life because you weren't present.
- You delayed evacuating, and the disaster struck.
- You failed to reconcile with someone, and now it's no longer possible.

In each case, you might hear the dreaded words: "Too late."

While these situations differ in severity, there is one scenario where "too late" has eternal consequences: failing to profess faith in Jesus during this life.

Ed Elliott studied all the red letters of Jesus and revealed an intriguing truth: Jesus spoke about Heaven far more frequently than Hell. Roughly 10 percent of His words refer to Heaven, compared to only 3 percent that mention Hell.[26] Yet, the fact that He addressed Hell at all, and with such urgency, underscores its eternal significance.

Jesus wasn't trying to inspire fear but to awaken hearts to the reality of eternity. Both Heaven and Hell are real, and the choices we make in this life have profound, everlasting consequences. This balance of hope and warning is vividly illustrated in the Parable of the Rich Man and Lazarus, where Jesus masterfully calls His listeners to consider their priorities and prepare for eternity.

THE RICH MAN AND LAZARUS

> "There was a rich man who was dressed in purple and fine linen and lived in luxury every day. At his gate was laid a beggar named Lazarus, covered with sores and longing to eat what fell from the rich man's table. Even the dogs came and licked his sores.
>
> "The time came when the beggar died and the angels carried him to Abraham's side. The rich man also died and was buried. In Hades, where he was in torment, he looked up and saw Abraham far away, with Lazarus by his side. So he called to him, 'Father Abraham, have pity on me and send Lazarus to dip the tip of his finger in water and cool my tongue, because I am in agony in this fire.'
>
> "But Abraham replied, 'Son, remember that in your lifetime you received your good things, while Lazarus received bad things, but now he is comforted here and you are in agony. And besides all this, between us and you a great chasm has been set in place, so that those who want to go from here to you cannot, nor can anyone cross over from there to us.'"
> **Luke 16:19-26**

From the start, Jesus contrasts two men: one rich, dressed in purple and fine linen, living a life of luxury; the other, Lazarus, a poor beggar, covered in sores and longing for scraps from the rich man's table. Even the dogs showed Lazarus more compassion than the rich man did.

It's significant that Jesus gives Lazarus a name, something unique among His parables. The rich man remains nameless, perhaps as a reminder that worldly wealth and status hold no weight in eternity.

When both men die, their fates are reversed. Lazarus is carried by angels to Abraham's side, a place of comfort. The rich man, however, finds himself in torment in Hades, another name for Hell, longing for a drip of cool water to hit his tongue. A far cry from where each man found themselves in life.

The rich man's cries for relief reveal the stark reality of his situation: It's too late. The choices he made in life, to live in selfish luxury without regard for others, have eternal consequences.

It's important to note that this parable isn't about salvation through good works or giving to the poor. Scripture is clear: We are saved by grace through faith in Jesus. As John 5:24 says, **"Very truly I tell you, whoever hears my word and believes him who sent me has eternal life and will not be judged but has crossed over from death to life." John 5:24**

However, for those of us who believe, the way we live and how we use our resources matter deeply. If we truly grasp the reality of eternity, it should shape how we prioritize our time, money, and relationships.

A PLEA FOR THE LIVING

Realizing that his own fate is sealed, the once rich but now forever poor man shifts his concern to his family.

> **"He answered, 'Then I beg you, father, send Lazarus to my family, for I have five brothers. Let him warn them, so that they will not also come to this place of torment.'**

> **"Abraham replied, 'They have Moses and the Prophets; let them listen to them.'**
>
> **"'No, father Abraham,' he said, 'but if someone from the dead goes to them, they will repent.'**
>
> **"He said to him, 'If they do not listen to Moses and the Prophets, they will not be convinced even if someone rises from the dead.'"** Luke 16:27-31

The formerly rich man's plea underscores a sobering truth: Some people will refuse to believe, even in the face of miraculous evidence. This prophecy comes to life later in the Gospel narrative, as another man aptly named Lazarus is raised from the dead—and still, many do not believe. Even more strikingly, Jesus Himself would rise from the dead, and yet some hearts would remain hardened.

For those of us who believe in Jesus, this parable is a call to action. We know the hope of Heaven, but that hope comes with responsibility. How we steward our time, our talents, and our resources matters.

It's easy to get caught up in the comforts of this world, but Jesus reminds us to keep an eternal perspective. Instead of living sumptuously, we're called to live generously, using our resources to bless others and advance God's Kingdom.

From a spiritual perspective, we are the "rich" ones, holding the bread of life. How can we keep this treasure to ourselves when there's a world desperate for even crumbs?

This story challenges us to think beyond ourselves. Is there someone you know and love who doesn't believe in Jesus? Are we stewarding what we've been given with eternity in mind? Are we living as if Heaven and Hell are real?

The words "too late" are some of the hardest to hear. But for those who trust in Jesus, there's still time to live in a way that reflects His heart and shares His hope with the world. Let's not waste the opportunities we've been given.

PREP DAY

Yesterday you prayed about a gift that you can give away. Tomorrow you will be encouraged to give your gift away.

Write down the gift you are feeling led to give tomorrow. You can write the amount and who you'd like to give the gift to. It can be a person, an organization, or your local church.

AMOUNT: _____

RECIPIENT: _____

As you write your potential gift down, pause and pray. In your prayer, ask God these three questions.

1. Is my gift generous?
2. Is my gift sacrificial?
3. Is my gift obedient?

#GIVINGCHALLENGE

- If the answers are "yes," then ask God to guide you in staying faithful to your decision.

- If the answers are "maybe," consider if God is asking you to give more.

- If the answers are "no," practice writing a higher number until you feel confident that what you are giving is generous, sacrificial, and obedient.

Let your giving reflect an eternal perspective, knowing that every act of generosity has the power to make a difference for His Kingdom.

DAY 18

GIVING THAT MATTERS

> "Truly I tell you, whatever you did for one of the least of these brothers of mine, you did for me."
>
> Matthew 25:40b

Whenever I take a spiritual gifts test, mercy often ranks low for me. Ugh. (If you've never taken one, visit **WWW.SPIRITUALGIFTS.ME** to take the free test we created!) This reveals that often I don't care as much as I should. But, instead of shrugging it off as just "that's how I am," I can do something about it.

Hopefully, throughout this book, you've seen that if your heart isn't naturally invested in something, but you know it should be, there's a way to change that. Our theme verse for the book reminds us that where you put your treasure, your heart will follow. If you want to care more about something, start by putting your resources like your time, energy, and especially your money, into it.

As stewards of all God has entrusted to us, aligning our giving with His heart is how we grow to love what He loves. Today, let's explore what God cares about most and how we can reflect His priorities as generous stewards. In their book *True Riches*, John Cortines and Gregory Baumer highlight three key areas where God's heart is clearly revealed.

❶ SERVE THE POOR (MERCY AND JUSTICE)

Throughout Scripture, God calls His people to care for the poor and oppressed. Jesus Himself emphasizes this responsibility in Matthew 25:34b-36,40b:

> **"'Come, you who are blessed by my Father; take your inheritance, the kingdom prepared for you since the creation of the world. For I was hungry and you gave me something to eat, I was thirsty and you gave me something to drink, I was a stranger and you invited me in, I needed clothes and you clothed me, I was sick and you looked after me, I was in prison and you came to visit me . . . Truly I tell you, whatever you did for one of the least of these brothers and sisters of mine, you did for me.'"**

Why do we care about the poor? Because God does. From Old Testament laws protecting widows and orphans to Jesus's ministry among society's most vulnerable, the Bible is clear: Believers are called to act justly, love mercy, and help those in need.

If you want to find where God is in the Bible, look for Him near the brokenhearted.

Psalm 34:18-19 says it like this: **"The LORD is close to the brokenhearted and saves those who are crushed in spirit. The righteous person may have many troubles, but the LORD delivers him from them all."**

As Cortines and Baumer write, "When our passion for giving to the needy is smaller than God's love for the needy, we face a faith-gap."[27] How you give to the poor may be complex, but the simple directive is all throughout the Bible. When you give to help the poor, you're not just meeting physical needs. You are reflecting God's heart.

② SAVE THE LOST (EVANGELISM)

When Jesus healed people, His work went beyond addressing their physical needs. His healing was holistic, reaching deeper to restore their spiritual condition as well. Why? Because as great as serving the physical needs of others is, the bigger issue that all of us struggle with is to be saved from our sins.

Some of Jesus's first red letters recorded in ministry were: **"The Spirit of the Lord is on me, because he has anointed me to proclaim good news to the poor. He has sent me to proclaim freedom for the prisoners and recovery of sight for the blind, to set the oppressed free, to proclaim the year of the Lord's favor." Luke 4:18-19**

God's desire is laid out even more clearly in 1 Timothy 2:4: **"[God] wants all people to be saved and to come to a knowledge of the truth."**

We're called to join this mission. Through the Great Commission (Matthew 28:19-20), some of Jesus's final red letters, He directs us to share the Good News and make disciples of all nations. When we give to spread the Gospel, whether through Bible translation, church planting, missionary support, or local evangelism, we align our hearts with God's mission to save the lost.

③ STRENGTHEN BELIEVERS (DISCIPLESHIP)

While God calls us to reach the lost, His mission doesn't stop there. True transformation happens as believers grow deeper in their faith and live out their calling as mature disciples. Jesus emphasizes this in the Great Commission:

> **"Teach them to obey everything that I have told you to do." Matthew 28:20a (ERV)**

#GIVINGCHALLENGE

This is where the Church plays a crucial role.

Jesus established the Church. In Matthew 16:18b (ESV), He said, **"I will build my church, and the gates of hell shall not prevail against it."** The Church is His idea. It will not fail. Some local churches may fail, but the Church never will.

He even went so far as to call the Church His bride (Ephesians 5:25-27). The Church is not just a building; it's a community of believers committed to making disciples. And Jesus is married to it. How much more can you love someone than by marrying them?

Sadly, today, a great movement is disengaging from the Church, and this is a work of the devil. He is trying to split up the great marriage. And, if I can offer one quick personal anecdote, I've never once in all my years ever seen a person who has left the Church grow in their faith. Not once.

The Church is where believers gather to become greater disciples. It's not the only place to grow in discipleship, for sure, but when the Church is doing its job, it is raising up disciples that make a difference in this world.

Giving to the Church is about more than supporting a local institution. It's about nurturing the faith of believers and fulfilling Christ's vision for His bride. When you give to the Church, know that you are putting your treasure and your heart into something Jesus deeply cares about and is forever committed to.

WHAT ABOUT 'OTHER' GIVING?

These three priorities—serving the poor, saving the lost, and strengthening believers—are clearly central to God's heart. But what about giving to other causes, like schools, hospitals, or the arts?

Jeremiah 29:7a reminds us to "seek the peace and prosperity of the city" we live in. Investing in our communities can reflect God's Kingdom, but it shouldn't come at the expense of His top priorities. Cortines and Baumer suggest allocating the majority of our giving to the "big three" while leaving room for other causes.

It's not wrong to give to libraries, alma maters, or technological research. These are good things. But here's the main point: Effective stewards align their actions with the heart of their owner. You are the steward. God is the owner.

One high-impact Christian donor, who gives only to Christian causes, does so not only because it reflects causes important to this person's heart. The donor says there are many others in the world, some who are not Christian, who will continue to fund non-Kingdom-related things.

The incredible thing about our Owner is His willingness to guide and help us. If you need wisdom, He promises to provide it generously. And as your heart becomes more like His, you'll naturally steward every part of your life, finances included, to more closely emulate your Owner.

Let's make the choice to invest in what matters most to God, and in doing so, create an impact that lasts for eternity.

#GIVINGCHALLENGE

CHALLENGE

GIVE DAY

Today you are being challenged to give your second of five gifts during these 40 days. Today's gift will make an eternal difference.

All this week, you have studied how Jesus gave eternally. You looked at your own life and how you spend your money, whether you live more as an owner or a steward. You've learned about the causes that matter to Jesus, and you prayed and planned to give a gift for eternal purposes. Give that gift today.

Led by God, give a gift that makes an eternal difference today.

DAY 19

LIVING FOR REWARDS

> "But store up for yourselves treasures in heaven."
> Matthew 6:20a

I got my first 100-percent cashmere sweater at age 22, and I was amazed. It felt next-level incredible! I thought, *I need more of these.* Over the next two years, I went a bit overboard and kept buying more and more. During those years while I was in seminary, I ran an eBay business and became skilled at finding great deals. In total, I had amassed a collection of about 15 cashmere sweaters.

Then, we received our first call out of seminary to plant a church in Florida.

Of all the things a new church planter in Florida needs, cashmere sweaters are not high on the list. So, I stuffed them away in a big box and threw them in a closet. All the way in the back. Not to be touched.

Fast forward 11 years when we moved to Omaha, Nebraska. All of a sudden, warm, fuzzy, winter clothes were a necessity again. When December hit, I excitedly opened my box of cashmere sweaters. I'd waited so long to wear them that I figured they might even be back in style!

I tried on my first sweater . . . only to find it riddled with tiny holes. Puzzled, I tried on another and another. Every sweater had been eaten through. My entire collection, destroyed. All because of these little pests called moths. Apparently, moths love to eat holes in expensive furs made of animal fibers, especially cashmere. Ugh.

I should have known better. Jesus warned us that earthly treasures, like my beloved sweaters, won't last. In Matthew 6:19, He says:

> **"Do not store up for yourselves treasures on earth, where moths and vermin destroy, and where thieves break in and steal."**

My sweaters taught me an important lesson about what Jesus once said: It's not that the things of this world are bad. They just don't last.

If you stopped here, you'd catch only part of what Jesus says. You might think He's telling us to avoid building up treasure for ourselves altogether. But that's not the case! In fact, in the very next words of Jesus, He encourages us to pursue treasure. Check it out, from Matthew 6:20:

> **"But store up for yourselves treasures in heaven, where moths and vermin do not destroy, and where thieves do not break in and steal."**

His challenge isn't about whether we should seek or store up treasure. Instead, he encourages us to think about where we're putting it. Jesus calls us to stop stockpiling treasures in temporary places and, instead, to invest in what truly lasts.

ETERNAL REWARDS

I've spent ample time this week reminding you that Heaven is your home. Not only is Heaven your home, but the Bible, especially through Jesus, is crystal-clear that how you live now in this world can impact your future heavenly home.

First things first. Eternal life is a gift given to you by Jesus, by grace, through faith. This is apart from your works. Need evidence of that? Open your Bible and read John 3:16 and Ephesians 2:8-9.

But did you know that about 40 times Jesus references something about eternal rewards based on our works?[28] Not 40 times in the Bible. Forty times just in the words of Jesus. It shows up throughout the rest of the Scriptures as well.

The only investment advice we have from Jesus, over and over again, is to not store up your treasure in this world, but to store it up in Heaven. As author Randy Alcorn says about money in his ground-breaking book *The Treasure Principle*, "You can't take it with you—but you can send it on ahead."[29]

Sometimes, Jesus will explicitly use the word "reward," and other times this idea will come in different forms. He speaks of accumulating treasure, receiving repayment, and being acknowledged as either the least or greatest in the kingdom. He also promises the reward of ruling alongside Him.

So, how can I earn these rewards?

By following Jesus and doing what He calls us to do.

In Matthew 10, a rich man was challenged by Jesus to live generously. He turned down the opportunity, and this sparked further conversation between the disciples and Jesus. The disciples were unsure how following Jesus and leaving the things of this world behind would work out in the end for them. Jesus assures them of this truth:

> "Truly I tell you, at the renewal of all things, when the Son of Man sits on his glorious throne, you who have followed me will also sit on twelve thrones, judging the twelve tribes of Israel. And everyone who has left houses or brothers or sisters or father or mother or wife or children or fields for my sake will receive a hundred times as much and will inherit eternal life. But many who are first will be last, and many who are last will be first." **Matthew 19:28-30**

The good news is that anytime you give up something of the world for the sake of following Jesus or sacrifice to further His Kingdom now, you have the promise of God that you will receive a hundredfold.

GOD'S WATCHING YOU!

One of the names of God in the Old Testament is "El Roi" which translates to "The God who sees me." Many times, we use the phrase "God's watching you," and it comes off more as a threat so you won't sin, especially in secret. But the flip side of "God's watching you" is true as well. If He's watching you, that means that even if every good thing you do doesn't come with recognition today, in the future, somehow, it'll work out even better for you.

This is true for your generous acts as well. Jesus says this in Matthew 6:2-4:

> "So when you give to the needy, do not announce it with trumpets, as the hypocrites do in the synagogues and on the streets, to be honored by

others. Truly I tell you, they have received their reward in full. But when you give to the needy, do not let your left hand know what your right hand is doing, so that your giving may be in secret. Then your Father, who sees what is done in secret, will reward you."

When you are generous to the needy, not only do you give them help for today, but you can store up rewards for yourself in Heaven. Talk about a win-win!

Admittedly, I don't fully understand what heavenly rewards will be like. But just because I don't fully understand it doesn't make it false. This is where faith comes in. Faith says that in some way, shape, and form, the little and the big things we do in this world will impact eternity.

Anything we try to hang onto here will be lost, but the things we do to bring God's Kingdom to this world right now, somehow will never stop paying dividends for us. I don't have much investment advice in this book, but the idea of eternal rewards, for those who have faith in the Lord, is the best investment Jesus says you can make.

Your good works not only can impact the eternal outcome of others, but they can impact your future as well. Fill your heavenly bank account today and one day, Jesus promises you, you'll be rewarded far greater than you can even imagine.

#GIVINGCHALLENGE

CHALLENGE

WRAP-UP DAY

Today, as we wrap up the Giving Eternally week, I pray you live more as a steward and less as an owner. Spend some time reflecting on your gift, and how you can keep trading ownership for stewardship in your life.

If you gave yesterday, how did it feel?

_____

_____

What would it look like to permanently trade ownership for stewardship in your life?

_____

_____

What was one major takeaway, feeling, or lesson that you received from this week's devotions and challenges?

_____

_____

19/40

DAYS 20-26

OF THE 40-DAY CHALLENGE

WEEK 4:
GIVING ABUN

TRADING SCARCITY FOR ABUNDANCE

"To whom much is given, much shall be required."

Luke 12:48b (RGT)

DAY 20

GOOD AND BAD EYES

> "The eye is the lamp of the body. If your eyes are healthy, your whole body will be full of light. But if your eyes are unhealthy, your whole body will be full of darkness."
>
> Matthew 6:22-23a

Imagine it's the year 4024 AD, and some people are planning a party with a throwback theme: 2020s in America. Intrigued, they dive into historical research to learn about how parties were celebrated back then. They come across a description of a party from 2024 featuring Gen Z characters. It reads like this:

"Jaden walked into a party, feeling like the main character. His drip was immaculate, head-to-toe snatched, and people couldn't stop commenting, 'Yo, your outfit slays!' He gave a subtle smirk, thinking, *No cap, I really did that.* The vibes were immaculate, with music that absolutely slapped, and everyone was on their A-game, passing the vibe check. When someone asked about his shoes, he flexed, 'They're custom, highkey exclusive, not cheugy.'

"Later, Jaden noticed Mia sitting in the corner, looking lowkey bored. He walked over with some rizz, saying, 'This party's bussin', but you're giving main character energy just sitting here.' She laughed, spilling the tea about her midday at work, and her coworker told her to touch grass. They both agreed the night hit different when the music switched to an old-school track. By the end of the party, Jaden knew this wasn't an L. It was a big W."[30]

Imagine stumbling upon that party description 2,000 years from now. Without understanding the cultural context, the words might feel like a foreign language. For some of you, those two paragraphs may seem more like you're reading a story from the 4020s because you are not in or around Gen Z culture much today. Words like "cheugy" and phrases like "touch grass" only make sense when you know the underlying values and humor of Gen Z culture.

The same is true when we approach Scripture. Just like modern slang reflects deeper cultural values, Jesus's expressions carry a richness that can be lost without understanding the context behind them. One of those examples is in our red letters for today when Jesus talks about "healthy" and "unhealthy" eyes. He isn't just talking about physical sight. There's something more happening culturally that we need to understand to grasp the deeper truth that may not jump off the page. So, let's check it out.

IF YOUR EYES ARE HEALTHY . . .

> **"If your eyes are healthy, your whole body will be full of light. But if your eyes are unhealthy, your whole body will be full of darkness." Matthew 6:22b-23a**

In Hebrew culture, the phrases "having a good eye" and "having a bad eye" were idioms with meanings that went beyond their literal interpretation. A "good eye" symbolized generosity and an abundance mindset, while a "bad eye" represented stinginess and a scarcity mindset.[31] This cultural nuance is why many Bible translations include footnotes next to the words "healthy" and "unhealthy" in Matthew 6:22-23. These notes suggest there is a deeper meaning to the words than what appears on the surface.

Jesus's words here are less about physical sight and more about one's mindset toward resources. It makes sense, too, because these red letters directly follow our theme verse for the entire book: **"For where your treasure is, there your heart will be also."** Together, these teachings emphasize the importance of viewing the world and our resources through the lens of abundance, not scarcity.

You view life through a lens that is uniquely yours—this is your mindset.

Your mindset determines so much of how you live and what you do. Just like in Jesus's day, it's common today for people to either adopt an abundance or a scarcity mindset.

SCARCITY OR ABUNDANCE MINDSET?

What's your mindset like? Do you typically operate with an abundance mindset or a scarcity mindset? In the challenge for today, you'll explore this further.

#GIVINGCHALLENGE

But why does it even matter?

Because what takes place in your mind and heart internally will naturally be reflected in your actions and behavior externally.

Jesus reminds us that a scarcity mindset is an unhealthy way to view the world. If you are unhealthy on the inside, you will be unhealthy on the outside. When your internal mindset and external actions are unhealthy, to put it frankly, you will not live the happy and meaningful life that Jesus called you to live.

Jesus spoke often about the posture of our hearts, and how it affects everything we do. When we adopt a mindset of abundance—believing that God is always at work, providing, and sustaining us—our lives reflect that faith. Let today be a reminder that you don't have to live in fear of scarcity. You were made for more, and the good work God started in you will never be hindered by lack. He has, is, and will give you everything that you need, and more. Embrace this promise. Live out of this reality. And, as you do, you will not only live a more joy-filled life, but you'll help others experience the same.

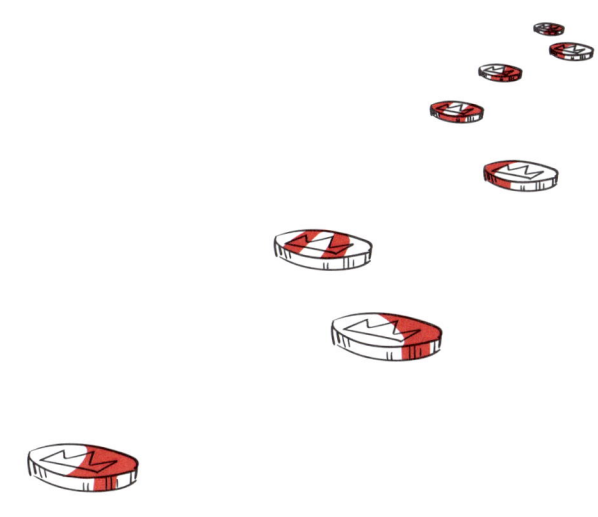

CHALLENGE

SCARCITY OR ABUNDANCE MINDSET CHECK

Place a checkmark next to the statement that best describes you. Mark which statement reflects your current mindset—not who you aspire to be, but how you're living right now.

☐ You think there will never be enough.	☐ You think there will always be more.
☐ You view work as a competition in which you must fight to stay ahead.	☐ You see work as a collaboration in which everyone can succeed together.
☐ You worry about the future.	☐ You have hope for the future.
☐ You think you deserve more credit.	☐ You desire to give credit to others.
☐ You see all that you have and believe you've earned it.	☐ You see everything you have as a gift given to you from God.
☐ You are naturally suspicious of others.	☐ You believe the best about others.
☐ You desire more.	☐ You enjoy what you have.

#GIVINGCHALLENGE

☐ You want to keep and store what you have.	☐ You want to share what you have.
☐ You live with fear.	☐ You live with trust.
☐ You see opportunities shrinking and worry about missing out.	☐ You see opportunities expanding and believe in creating more.
☐ You live in constant comparison.	☐ You are content with what you have.
☐ You see the glass half empty.	☐ You see the glass half full.
☐ You expect outcomes to worsen.	☐ You expect outcomes to get better.

Count the number of checkmarks on the right side and circle the number below. If your number is low, you are likely living with a scarcity mindset. If your number is high, you're operating with an abundance mindset.

Scarcity 1 2 3 4 5 6 7 8 9 10 11 12 13 **Abundance**

Whatever your number might be, set a goal to improve by at least two or three points. What action or next steps can you take this week to get better? Write it down and act on it.

20/40

DAY 21

THE CURRENCY OF GRACE

"It is finished."

John 19:30b

One of the difficult things about writing a book about the generosity of Jesus is that while we have many of His words, we don't have much information, if any, about how Jesus actually spent, received, or earned money.

We know He worked for His dad in the "craftsmanship" business, likely working with both wood and stone. I can assume that Jesus earned money for that work. But we don't know what His net worth was, or if He ever left any money on deposit. He didn't appear to have any equity in a home and had no money for retirement, which wasn't even invented until centuries later and then popularized in America in the early 1900s.

Just because we don't see Jesus using the currency of His day doesn't mean that Jesus didn't operate with incredible financial wisdom and understanding. In fact, you could make the case that the last recorded words of Jesus on the cross in John could be understood from a financial perspective.

John 19:30 says, **"When he had received the drink, Jesus said, 'It is finished.' With that, he bowed his head and gave up his spirit."**

The Greek word *"tetelestai"* is a perfect tense verb typically translated as "It is finished." A perfect tense verb means that the action was completed in the past but also implies that it will have continuing results.

The meaning of this word can and certainly does imply that when Jesus died on the cross, His saving act was completed. He came for a set purpose, to save humanity from our sins, and it was done, at this moment, once and for all. Hallelujah!

However, as I've written before in my work *Forgiving Challenge*, there is an alternative definition of *tetelestai* that is important for our purposes in this book. "Interestingly, the word *tetelestai* was also written on business documents or receipts in New Testament times to indicate that a bill had been paid in full."[32]

When those at the crucifixion heard this word from Jesus, they would have understood it from a financial sense. Not only is the work completed, but Jesus is saying that something in that moment was paid in full. What was it?

Friends, it's the very heart of the Gospel. Jesus came into this world on a rescue mission to get back His most prized possession—you and me. Our sin had separated us from our relationship with God. For the relationship to be restored, there had to be a payment. But not just any payment. It had to be His blood.

Blood is the most valuable currency in the Bible for what matters most.

Let me explain.

In the Old Testament, whenever someone sinned, they would sacrifice an innocent animal, like a lamb or bull, as a substitute to cover their sin. The animal's blood represented life and took on the penalty the person deserved, showing that sin required a costly payment. This sacrificial system pointed ahead to the ultimate need for a perfect, once-and-for-all sacrifice. This was the need that Jesus came to fulfill.

So, would Jesus be willing to pay this price? Heck yes, He would! The blood of innocent animals was a temporary payment, but when Jesus shed His blood, His was the permanent payment.

Jesus deposited every ounce of blood He had on a Friday at 3 p.m. If large financial deposits were the same back then as they are today, the bigger the payment, the longer it would have taken to clear. But this massive, monumental payment didn't even need the full weekend to clear. On Sunday morning, as Jesus rose from the dead, the payment cleared, which is why the Church gathers on that day to celebrate the completed work of the cross. I know normal banking hours today are Monday through Friday, but let's just say God gets a good portion of His accounting done on Sundays!

When you receive this gift of grace, it doesn't matter what hour or day it is. It is fully paid for by Jesus so that when you say "yes" to it, it is instantly deposited into your heavenly bank account. You receive eternal life in the presence of God in perpetuity.

Jesus fully paid for you. He gave everything. He held nothing back. So, while we don't have a record of Jesus using the currency of that day, you could argue that His blood is the most valuable currency the world has ever seen. And Jesus dropped every single ounce of it to pay the ultimate price to get you and me back.

He must think you are valuable. Value is determined by the price you're willing to pay. And He paid an abundant, impossible, unbelievable amount to get you. He paid with a currency that has far greater value than any amount of riches you or I could ever accumulate.

#GIVINGCHALLENGE

"He entered the Most Holy Place once for all by his own blood, thus obtaining eternal redemption."

HEBREWS 9:12B

#GIVINGCHALLENGE

BYOB PARTY

Imagine the throne room scene in Hebrews, chapters 9 and 10. Jesus, at His ascension, re-enters heaven. He doesn't come with the blood of bulls or goats but with His own blood. This is what I like to call a "Bring Your Own Blood" (BYOB) party. Hebrews 9:12b says, **"He entered the Most Holy Place once for all by his own blood, thus obtaining eternal redemption."**

Unlike earthly priests who offered daily sacrifices that could never fully remove sin, Jesus offered one final, perfect sacrifice—Himself. Hebrews 10:12-13 describes how Jesus sat down at God's right hand, signaling that His work was finished and our redemption fully secured.

So, picture this: Jesus, the Lamb who was slain, victoriously presents His own blood as payment to the Father, not the blood of any random sacrifice. He reclaims His place on the throne, while His enemies are now His footstool—a completed action with ongoing power.

In a sense, Jesus is saying, *"Paid in full. For _____ (fill in your name), for everyone."* Then, He sits on His throne, having completed His mission, interceded for His people, and defeated death. As He is seated, He is greeted with the repeated refrain of "Holy, Holy, Holy."

Wow! What a God! What a hero!

Jesus gave out of His abundance of riches so that you and I could be made right. We, who were spiritually bankrupt, are set free by the blood of Jesus. The Bible says that when God the Father looks at you, He sees Jesus, the perfect, spotless, and innocent Lamb of God. You have been given much.

While we have no idea how Jesus handled His earthly currency, He knew exactly what His *heavenly* currency was worth . . . and He chose to spend THAT on us. How incredible is that?

CHALLENGE

LOOK TO JESUS

Read John 19:16-30. When Jesus said, "It is finished," on the cross, what do you think He meant? How does this show that His mission to save us was fully completed?

_____

_____

_____

In the Old Testament, sacrifices were made with the blood of animals to cover sins temporarily. Why was Jesus's sacrifice so much more powerful and final?

_____

_____

_____

How does knowing that Jesus gave everything for us help you understand how much He loves you?

_____

_____

_____

21/40

DAY 22

THE NEVER-ENDING CHASE

> "The thief comes only to steal and kill and destroy. I came that they may have life and have it abundantly."
>
> John 10:10 (ESV)

Our world constantly tells us we don't have enough, and few things amplify that message like slot machines. Even if you've never played one, their influence extends far beyond the casino floor.

Michael Easter, in *Scarcity Brain*, reveals their staggering impact. Today, slot machines generate up to 85 percent of casino profits, or $30 billion annually in the U.S.—more than we spend on movies, books, and music combined. Yet, they were once a minor attraction. Before the 1980s, card and dice games made 10 times as much money. The turning point? Easter argues it was the Atari video game system.[33]

Las Vegas executives noticed kids glued to video games, hooked by wins and losses without real rewards. They applied these principles to slot machines, adding digital screens, multiple betting lines, and frequent small "wins" to trigger the brain's reward system. Winning 50 cents on a $1 bet is still labeled a "win," tricking players into feeling good despite a loss.

Designers perfected the experience by slowing reels for suspense, flashing lights for excitement, and extending anticipation. Research shows dopamine spikes most during the chase, not the reward. Winning feels good, but chasing the win feels even better.

Modern video games, far beyond the simplicity of Atari, also exploit this psychology. Games like *Candy Crush* have found the brain reacts strongly to near-misses, convincing players to keep going and keep spending because victory seems just out of reach.

This addictive psychology isn't confined to video games and casinos.

Social media thrives on unpredictable likes and comments. Apps like Temu (the most downloaded App of 2024) gamify shopping with spin-to-win rewards. Trading platforms like Robinhood make day trading accessible, despite high failure rates. Streaming services autoplay the next episode, fitness trackers gamify health, and dating apps turn swiping into a reward cycle. Political antics thrive on unpredictable behavior, which always captures media attention and captivates audiences.

FALLING FOR LIES

In 1928, Edward Bernays, a pioneer in the world of public relations, observed:

> "In almost every act of our daily lives . . . we are dominated by the relatively small number of persons . . . who understand the mental processes and social patterns of the masses . . . we are governed, our minds molded, our tastes formed, our ideas suggested, largely by [people] we have never heard of . . . It is they who pull the wires which control the public mind."[34]

A century later, these "wires" are even more sophisticated, shaping habits and decisions in ways we barely notice.

Falling for these "wires" is taking a toll on our mental health. Despite living in history's most prosperous times, we face unprecedented levels of worry, anxiety, and stress. Look at any list of major worries and you will find money and finance always at the top. We're "blessed and stressed," a paradox made possible only when we believe the world's lies.

Jesus reminds us of this battle in our red letters for today: **"The thief comes only to steal and kill and destroy."** The thief presents the world as if it's all there is, convincing us that the key to a happy life is found chasing more and more.

Make no mistake. You are being lied to. The adversary works hard to keep you chasing. The lie many believe is that happiness is just one step away. Take the vacation, and you'll find rest. Eat the meal, and you'll feel satisfied. Drink the wine, and you'll find relief. Buy the car, and you'll feel accomplished. Get the promotion, and you'll finally feel secure. Hit the jackpot, and euphoria will be yours.

But here's the truth: If the adversary has got you chasing, he's already won. The outcome of the chase, whether you win or lose, doesn't matter to the enemy.

This endless pursuit of "more" isn't new. People have wrestled with it for centuries. Even King Solomon, the richest man in history, reflected on the futility of wealth in his final years:

> **Whoever loves money never has enough; whoever loves wealth is never satisfied with their income. This too is meaningless. As goods increase, so do those who consume them . . . The sleep of a laborer is sweet, whether they eat little or much, but as for the rich, their abundance permits them no sleep. Ecclesiastes 5:10-12**

You can chase and win, only to feel emptier than ever. Or you can chase and lose, hitting rock-bottom. Either way, the scarcity mindset keeps you captive, whether you're rich or poor.

LIVING FOR TRUTH

The devil may be our adversary, but thankfully Jesus is fighting against him and for us. If the devil presents the world to you, then Jesus presents the Kingdom of Heaven to you: **"I came that they may have life and have it abundantly."**

#GIVINGCHALLENGE

Kingdom People think differently. As we've discussed in detail in this book already, we know this world is important, but it's not all there is, so it's foolish to fall for the enemy's lies. When we live with this mindset, we realize we have everything we need and can stop chasing.

The good news is you don't need to accumulate, chase, or earn more. Your time to climb ladders is done. Your identity and place in God's Kingdom are given to you by Jesus as a free gift of grace.

Life isn't about accumulating possessions or chasing temporary pleasures. It's about receiving the gift of eternal life, which frees you from the pressures of this world. God's grace is more than enough for you. It's given abundantly, so you can live with the right mindset.

Michael Easter, in *Scarcity Brain*, notes:

> "We now have an abundance—some might say an overload—of the things we've evolved to crave—things like food . . . possessions . . . information . . . mood adjusters . . . and influence—Yet we're still programmed to think and act as if we don't have enough. As if we're still in those ancient times of scarcity . . . The science shows that our scarcity brain doesn't always make sense in our modern world of abundance. It now often works against us, and outside forces are exploiting it to influence our decisions."[35]

Although Easter doesn't write from a Christian perspective, his conclusion aligns with Jesus's teachings—another example of science catching up to what Jesus has always said. In Easter's words, "Permanent change and lasting satisfaction in life is finding enough. Not too much. Not too little."[36]

In Jesus, you have enough. Everything you need. Not too much. Not too little.

CHALLENGE

TRACK YOUR MONEY

Assess your material possessions today.

Go through your items one by one and list them under the appropriate category. Mark the column (Keep, Sell, or Donate) for each item based on its condition, value, and usefulness to you.

- **Keep:** Items you love or use regularly.
- **Sell:** Items in good condition that are valuable and could earn money.
- **Donate:** Items still useful but no longer needed, which could help others.

	KEEP	SELL	DONATE
CLOTHING + ACCESSORIES			
Clothes (e.g., T-shirts, Jackets)	☐	☐	☐
Shoes	☐	☐	☐
Jewelry	☐	☐	☐
ELECTRONICS			
Electronics (e.g., Phone, Laptop)	☐	☐	☐
HOME ESSENTIALS			
Kitchen Appliances	☐	☐	☐
Furniture (e.g., Chair, Table)	☐	☐	☐
Art/Décor (e.g., Wall Art, Vases)	☐	☐	☐
ENTERTAINMENT			
Books	☐	☐	☐
Toys/Games	☐	☐	☐

#GIVINGCHALLENGE

	KEEP	SELL	DONATE
HOBBY/LEISURE			
Collectibles (e.g., Stamps, Cards)	☐	☐	☐
Sports Equipment	☐	☐	☐
HOBBY/PRACTICAL			
Tools (e.g., Hammer, Drill)	☐	☐	☐
MISCELLANEOUS			
Unused Gifts	☐	☐	☐

❶ What items were the hardest to part with, and why?
- Did you struggle with sentimental value, the idea of "just in case," or the money originally spent on the item? What does this reveal about your relationship with material possessions?

❷ How does decluttering and giving away items impact your perspective on generosity?
- Did the process help you realize you have more than enough? How might donating useful items shift your mindset toward sharing and blessing others with what you no longer need?

❸ How can this exercise shape your future spending habits?
- After seeing how many things you're willing to let go of, are there areas where you might be more intentional with future purchases? Could you focus on buying less, investing in quality, or giving more instead of accumulating?

22/40

DAY 23

FEAR OF MISSING OUT

"Don't be afraid of missing out. You're my dearest friends! The Father wants to give you the very kingdom itself."
Luke 12:32 (MSG)

As I walked into the car dealership with my son Nathan, I couldn't help but feel like George Costanza from *Seinfeld*, ready to coach Jerry Seinfeld through the classic car-buying hustle. Nathan, having diligently saved for years, was ready to buy his first car, and I was determined to help him get the best deal without falling for any sales tricks.

Before stepping onto the lot, we set our budget and strategy: Get the salesman to share their lowest price first, counter with something lower, and settle somewhere in between. Sure enough, the salesman used every trick in the book. He highlighted the rarity of the car, stalled to "talk to his manager," and emphasized how quickly it would sell. But in the end, Nathan drove off with the car he wanted for less than the highest price we were willing to pay. Victory!

Looking back, I realized how much "scarcity marketing" played a role in that transaction. The urgency wasn't just about the car itself. It was about creating the fear of missing out.

Scarcity marketing is everywhere once you know how to spot it.

Think about the slogans you've likely encountered:

- ACT NOW—SUPPLIES ARE RUNNING OUT!
- LIMITED-TIME BONUS—ONLY AVAILABLE TODAY!
- FINAL HOURS TO SAVE BIG!
- EXCLUSIVE OFFER ENDS TONIGHT!
- ONCE-IN-A-LIFETIME DEAL—DON'T MISS OUT!
- ONLY [X] LEFT IN STOCK—ORDER NOW!
- SPECIAL EARLY ACCESS FOR A LIMITED TIME!
- HURRY! OFFER EXPIRES AT MIDNIGHT.
- LAST CHANCE TO CLAIM YOUR DISCOUNT!

These messages aren't just words. They're designed to trigger action. Companies amplify the effect with visual tactics: countdown timers, flashy banners, spin-to-win wheels, expiring rewards, and push notifications urging you to act immediately. The goal? To make you feel that if you don't act now, you'll lose out forever.

Why does this work so well? Because scarcity marketing exploits our fear of missing out, a fear that's become more prevalent in today's hyper-connected world.

FYRE FLOP

If there's one event that truly embodies the Fear of Missing Out (FOMO), it's the Fyre Festival of 2017. Billed as a high-end, luxury music festival on a private island in the Bahamas, it promised attendees the ultimate exclusive experience: private villas, gourmet meals, and performances by top-tier artists. The festival was hyped as a can't-miss event for the elite, and its marketing campaign was pure genius.

Using influencer endorsements from models and celebrities, stunning visuals of pristine beaches, and the allure of exclusivity, the campaign didn't just grab attention. It created obsession. People weren't just buying tickets to a music festival; they were buying into a dream. And they paid outrageous amounts of money to do it.

But when attendees arrived, that dream turned into a nightmare. Instead of luxury accommodations, they found FEMA tents hastily pitched on a gravel lot. The promised gourmet meals? A sad cheese sandwich in a Styrofoam container. Headlining musical acts pulled out at the last minute, and many of the influencers who "endorsed" the event never actually planned to attend. Chaos ensued as stranded festivalgoers scrambled to find flights home.

The mastermind behind it all, Billy McFarland, was eventually convicted of fraud and served four years in prison. Shockingly, he's already planning a second Fyre Festival. My advice? Don't fall for it.

The Fyre Festival is more than just a story about a failed event. It's a textbook example of how scarcity and exclusivity can be powerful marketing tools. The urgency to buy now, the fear of missing out on something others seem to be experiencing, and the perception that "everyone important" is involved all work together to create a frenzy. This is what's known as bandwagon marketing. Marketers rely on the idea that nothing draws a crowd like the appearance of a crowd.

KINGDOM ABUNDANCE

In a world driven by scarcity and fear of missing out, Jesus offers us a radically different perspective.

Luke 12:32 (MSG) says it plainly: **"Don't be afraid of missing out. You're my dearest friends! The Father wants to give you the very kingdom itself."**

What an extraordinary promise. While the world shouts, "Hurry, or you'll miss your chance," Jesus whispers, "You don't have to scramble or fear. Everything you truly need is already yours in Me." He shifts our focus from the fleeting and the temporary to the eternal and the abundant.

The Kingdom of God doesn't operate on scarcity. It's built on abundance. God's grace, love, and provision are not limited resources. You don't need to compete for them or worry that someone else's gain means your loss. Unlike the empty promises of marketing campaigns, Jesus delivers on every word. He doesn't bait us with false urgency or exclusivity; He invites us into a relationship where His blessings are limitless and eternal.

Jesus doesn't invite you to a three-day festival on a private island. He invites you through His grace to an eternal future where the gates are made of pearls and the streets of gold. This future in and through Jesus will far outshine even the best fantasy and dream you can come up with in this world.

When we live in the security of Jesus's abundance, we're freed from the grip of FOMO. We don't have to chase after every deal, event, or trend, fearing we'll be left behind. Instead, we can rest in the assurance that we already have the greatest treasure: life with God. Scarcity may be the language of the world, but abundance is the language of Jesus.

His Kingdom is never out of stock.

PRAY DAY

Every week you will be challenged to pray about your giving. As you discern what/how to give each week, you will never be told a specific amount. Our recommendation for you is to bring all these decisions before God through prayer.

Here are the prayer steps we're asking you to follow each week:

1 Acknowledge that God is most generous and thank Him for His provision.

2 Ask God how you can be generous this week.

3 Listen for His direction. For specifics on how to hear God's voice, check out this blog: "3 Questions to Help You Know if You Are Hearing God's Voice."

4 Be obedient. When God is leading you to give, follow His lead and trust Him fully.

#GIVINGCHALLENGE

If you need more direction, here's a prayer you can pray this week:

Heavenly Father,

I come before You today with an open heart, asking You to guide me in my giving. You are the Ultimate Provider, and all I have comes from You. You have abundantly provided for me, and with You leading me, I lack nothing. So, Lord, what would You have me give? How can I give out of my abundance to make a difference in the lives of others?

God, I'm quieting my heart and listening for Your direction. Give me discernment to recognize Your voice now and clarity to follow where You lead.

Consider pausing in silence for a minute or two.

Lord, I choose to trust You. I will respond with obedience. I know that You see the bigger picture, that You have my best in mind, and that You will always provide for my needs. Help me to release any fear or hesitation, and to give with a joyful heart. May my giving be an act of worship that draws me closer to Your heart.

In Jesus's name,
Amen.

23/40

DAY 24

THE PARTICIPATION MIRACLE

> "You give them something to eat."
>
> **Matthew 14:16b**

For my dad's retirement from ministry, a member of our church gave him an incredible gift: an exclusive golf trip for him and a small group of his choosing. Thankfully, I made the list. Together, we experienced the opportunity of a lifetime, playing one of the world's most prestigious golf courses. Not once, not twice, but three days in a row. And as if that weren't enough, we stayed on the property and enjoyed every amenity the club had to offer, including unlimited FREE milkshakes! It was a weekend straight out of a dream and one I'll never forget.

The only thing that could have been better was my golf game.

That weekend taught me an important lesson: Who you know makes all the difference. I wasn't there because of anything I'd done. The only reason I got to set foot on that course, stay on the property, or enjoy those amenities was because 1) I'm the son of Mark Zehnder, and 2) I was with a friend of his who happened to be a member of the club. Without those connections, getting in would have been next to impossible.

Once we were on the property, all we had to do was mention the member's name. My name didn't carry any weight. But his name gave me access to one of the most extraordinary places I've ever been, along with some of the finest customer service I've ever experienced.

At that golf club, everything came down to who you know. And the same is true in life.

Who do you know? Because I knew a member—or more importantly, the member knew me—I could trust that I would be well taken care of.

Friends, not only do you know Jesus, but He knows you. And He always has your best interest at heart. Sometimes, what's best for you isn't just receiving from Him but being invited to give to others. God could accomplish everything Himself, but He chooses to work through us, His stewards, to bring His kingdom closer to this world.

One incredible example of this is found on a hillside, where resources were scarce.

THE FEEDING OF THE 5,000

This is one of the most famous miracles in the Bible and one of only two miracles (along with the resurrection) recorded in all four Gospels. Clearly, God wants us to pay attention to this story.

The miracle is found in Matthew 14. At this point, a large crowd had gathered, listening to Jesus for hours. He had already been healing their sick, but He wasn't finished with them yet. As evening approached, the disciples noticed a practical problem: The people were hungry, and there was no food. They said to Jesus:

> **"This is a remote place, and it's already getting late. Send the crowds away, so they can go to the villages and buy themselves some food."**
> **Matthew 14:15b**

The disciples' solution seemed logical. They recognized the scarcity of food and wanted to give people time to find something to eat. But Jesus had a different plan. **Jesus replied, "They do not need to go away. You give them something to eat." Matthew 14:16**

Imagine the disciples' shock. They must have thought, *What are we supposed to do? Feed thousands of people? With what? Doordash doesn't even deliver out this far.*

> **"We have here only five loaves of bread and two fish," they answered.**
> **Matthew 14:17**

According to other Gospel accounts, this small amount of food came from a boy's lunch. For years, I couldn't wrap my mind around how a boy could have packed five loaves of bread for a single meal. But now, as the parent of teenage boys, I get it.

Even so, a big lunch for one boy is still a minuscule amount of food when you're staring at a crowd of 15,000 to 20,000 including women and children. I can just imagine the disciples stressing the word "only" as they said it: *"We have here only five loaves and two fish."*

Scarcity-minded thinking often sounds like this: "I only have this." "It's just a little." "It's not enough."

For Jesus, what seems like "only" is more than enough for Him to accomplish the impossible.

#GIVINGCHALLENGE

"Bring them here to me," he said. And he directed the people to sit down on the grass. Taking the five loaves and the two fish and looking up to heaven, he gave thanks and broke the loaves. Then he gave them to the disciples, and the disciples gave them to the people. They all ate and were satisfied, and the disciples picked up twelve basketfuls of broken pieces that were left over. The number of those who ate was about five thousand men, besides women and children. Matthew 14:18-21

A LOT THROUGH A LITTLE

When the disciples trusted and obeyed Jesus, they saw God's miraculous provision firsthand. A crowd of 15,000 to 20,000 was fed with just five loaves and two fish. As if that wasn't enough, each disciple walked away with a basketful of leftovers, proving God's abundance.

When we trust Jesus, He not only meets our needs but goes above and beyond.

This story parallels God's provision for the Israelites in the wilderness. For 40 years, God rained down manna from heaven, providing bread six days a week. On the sixth day, they were instructed to collect double so they could rest on the Sabbath. But when some Israelites hoarded extra bread and operated with a scarcity mindset, forgetting who was providing for them daily, the bread spoiled.

The feeding of the 5,000 wasn't just a miracle of provision; it was also a miracle of participation. Both the disciples and the boy who brought his lunch played a role. While Jesus could have created the bread and fish out of thin air, He chose to work through ordinary people. He invited them to be stewards, offering their resources, both food and time, to join Him in accomplishing the miracle.

As stewards of God's resources, our role isn't to solve every problem on our own. Instead, it's to bring what we have in faith and trust God to do the rest. When we offer what we have and work together, God's abundance overflows in ways we could never achieve by ourselves.

The disciples began this story unsure of how things would work out. But as they participated in Jesus's plan, they didn't just witness the abundance. They experienced it firsthand.

This story reminds us that our God can do a lot with a little. When it comes to generosity, we are called to give from what we have, no matter how small it seems. In the hands of Jesus, even the smallest gift can be multiplied to bless others and reveal God's power in ways we never imagined.

Our God is the God of more than enough.

Better is a little in God's hands than a lot in your hands.

King Solomon reminds us of this truth: **"Better a little with the fear of the Lord than great wealth with turmoil." Proverbs 15:16**

When we trust God, we don't have to live with a scarcity mindset. Instead, we can give abundantly, knowing He will take care of us. Not just for a moment but for eternity. He knows your name.

And that, my friends, makes all the difference.

CHALLENGE

PREP DAY

Yesterday you prayed about a gift that you can give away. Tomorrow you will be encouraged to give your gift away.

Write down the gift you are feeling led to give tomorrow. You can write the amount and who you'd like to give the gift to. It can be a person, an organization, or your local church.

AMOUNT: _____

RECIPIENT: _____

As you write your potential gift down, pause and pray. In your prayer, ask God these three questions.

1 Is my gift generous?

2 Is my gift sacrificial?

3 Is my gift obedient?

- If the answers are "yes," then ask God to guide you in staying faithful to your decision.

- If the answers are "maybe," consider if God is asking you to give more.

- If the answers are "no," practice writing a higher number until you feel confident that what you are giving is generous, sacrificial, and obedient.

Let your giving reflect an eternal perspective, knowing that every act of generosity has the power to make a difference for His Kingdom.

24/40

DAY 25

LIVING LARGE

> "I am the good shepherd. The good shepherd lays down his life for the sheep."
> John 10:11

Do you ever feel like you lack something in life, like there's never enough?

One of the most powerful images of God in the Bible that combats this thinking is a shepherd. In John 10:11, just after inviting us to an abundant life, Jesus says, **"I am the good shepherd. The good shepherd lays down his life for the sheep."**

David, who wrote many of the Psalms, knew this image well. Before he was king of Israel, he was a shepherd, and in Psalm 23:1, he wrote, **"The Lord is my shepherd, I lack nothing."**

David's victory over Goliath highlights this truth. As a young shepherd, he stood up when no one else would. After hearing Goliath taunt the God of Israel, David, fresh from tending sheep, spoke to King Saul, who questioned his ability to fight.

When Saul doubted David, David didn't list any impressive feats showing why he was fit to fight Goliath. He didn't say, "I can defeat Goliath because I can bench press double my weight." He didn't have any karate skills learned from a sensei. Instead, he spoke of his qualifications as a shepherd. And side note, what follows are some of the most manly Bible verses ever!

But David said to Saul, "Your servant has been keeping his father's sheep. When a lion or a bear came and carried off a sheep from the flock, I went

> **after it, struck it and rescued the sheep from its mouth. When it turned on me, I seized it by its hair, struck it and killed it. Your servant has killed both the lion and the bear; this uncircumcised Philistine will be like one of them, because he has defied the armies of the living God. The LORD who rescued me from the paw of the lion and the paw of the bear will rescue me from the hand of this Philistine." 1 Samuel 17:34-37**

David's boldness came not from his strength, but from his trust in God's provision and protection. Jesus, like David, is our Good Shepherd. He laid down His life for us so we could experience abundant life. Everything we need to live abundantly is found in Him.

With God as our Good Shepherd, we can confidently say, "The Lord is my shepherd, I lack nothing." This mindset changes how we live. We no longer need to worry about creating our own safety nets because God has already provided one.

God didn't create you to live a lackluster life. He created you to live a "lacknothing" life.

When we recognize we lack nothing in Christ, we can be generous with what we have to impact others. This is exactly what Sasha Berscheid did.

OUT OF YOUR ABUNDANCE

Sasha found herself at rock bottom, leaning her head against a porcelain toilet, detoxing from alcoholism. She cried out, "God, save me from this. Help me, and I will be your vessel." God answered her prayer, and Sasha not only survived that weekend but began the hard work of recovery through Alcoholics Anonymous. Now, with over a decade of sobriety, she credits her victory to His faithfulness.

Sasha's promise to be God's vessel took shape in a remarkable way. Five years later, holding her two babies in her arms, her husband asked her a simple question,

"What do you want for Christmas?" In that moment, overwhelmed by gratitude for God's provision and holding her children close, she realized she didn't need or want anything. Everything she could have asked for, God had already provided. She had an abundance of blessings.

But her thoughts quickly turned outward: *What about the moms who don't have what I have?*

Instead of asking for a gift, Sasha chose to "adopt" a single mom for Christmas. She shared her idea in a local Omaha Moms Facebook group, hoping to help one woman. To her surprise, over 80 women responded, listing basic necessities like socks, diapers, and pull-ups. Moved by the need, Sasha took the lead, rallying friends and family to support all 80 women that first Christmas in 2019.

What started as a simple act of generosity grew into a nonprofit, Project Intentional, which by 2023 was providing essentials and hope to over 1,500 women.

Sasha's story shows how recognizing God's abundance in our lives leads to generosity.

Many life-changing missions begin with small, humble roots. Sasha's journey demonstrates how one person's willingness to serve can ripple through a community.

Through Project Intentional, Sasha fulfilled her promise to be God's vessel and found the abundant life He created for her to live. Her story challenges us all to use what we have to make a difference in the world. For more of Sasha's story, listen to the *Red Letter Disciple* podcast episode where I had the chance to interview her.[37]

So, what has God given to you?

#GIVINGCHALLENGE

LIVING LARGE BIBLICALLY

"Living large" is a popular American slang term for living like a wealthy and successful person. Surprisingly, the Bible talks about living large, too. King Solomon, David's son, gives us this wisdom:

> **The world of the generous gets larger and larger; the world of the stingy gets smaller and smaller. The one who blesses others is abundantly blessed; those who help others are helped. Proverbs 11:24-25 (MSG)**

Generosity helps you loosen your grip on material things and draw closer to your Good Shepherd. Every act of giving opens the door to blessings, both for you and others.

The mindset you choose—scarcity or abundance—affects your mental health. It's better to have great mental health and live with purpose, even if your net worth is low, than to suffer from anxiety and poor mental health despite having a high net worth.

When you give generously out of your abundance, you experience even more abundance. Financial blessings may not always follow your giving, but you'll find joy, happiness, and fulfillment knowing that your generosity is making an eternal impact.

The best way to "live large" biblically is to give generously. God isn't opposed to wealth. Rather, He's saying that true abundance comes from giving, not just gaining. Living large isn't about accumulating more for yourself; it's about sharing what you have to bless others. Paul wrote:

Command those who are rich in this present world not to be arrogant nor to put their hope in wealth, which is so uncertain, but to put their hope in God, who richly provides us with everything for our enjoyment. Command them to do good, to be rich in good deeds, and to be generous and willing to share. In this way they will lay up treasure for themselves as a firm foundation for the coming age, so that they may take hold of the life that is truly life. 1 Timothy 6:17-19

Jesus invites you into a life of abundance, trusting that God is your Good Shepherd. Ironically, the way you take hold of the abundant life is by letting go of what God puts in your hands.

You should live large. You should act like a wealthy person. Why? Because, in Christ, you lack nothing. You are rich. So, live large and be the best rich person you can be.

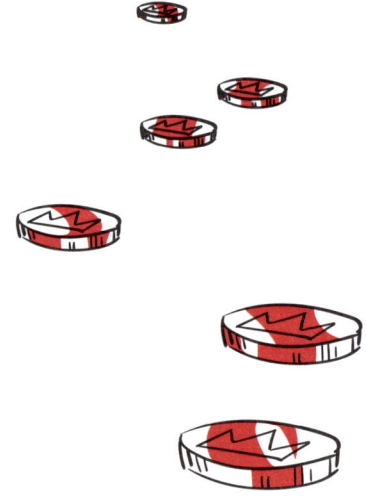

CHALLENGE

GIVE DAY

Today you are being challenged to give your third of five gifts during these 40 days. This gift will help you "live large" by living with an abundance mindset.

All this week, you have studied how Jesus gave abundantly to you. You have looked at how many material possessions you have, and assessed what you can live without, trading a scarcity mindset for an abundant mindset. That assessment may have left you with extra money or possessions to give away this week. After praying about what God wants you to do with the extra, give a gift today.

Led by God, give a gift out of your abundance today.

25/40

DAY 26

TRY IT

> "All these people gave their gifts out of their wealth; but she out of her poverty put in all she had to live on."
> Luke 21:4

Our mindset shapes our actions, and what happens internally inevitably shows externally. However, the reverse is also true: Sometimes the actions we take on the outside can reshape our internal attitudes. This dynamic is especially significant when moving from a scarcity mindset, a belief in limited resources, to an abundance mindset rooted in faith and generosity.

To live abundantly, we must sometimes act abundantly first.

Authors Peter Greer and Chris Horst, in their book *Rooting for Rivals*, explore the prevalence of scarcity thinking even among Christians. When interviewed on *The Red Letter Disciple Podcast*, Peter was asked how someone could transition from a scarcity to an abundance mindset. His answer was refreshingly simple: "Try it."[38]

Generosity is the best way to cultivate an abundance mindset. You can read about it, plan for it, and pray over it, but nothing compares to experiencing it firsthand. As Nike's slogan suggests, "Just do it."

John Mark Comer affirms this idea: "Generosity is a practice by which we index our heart from a scarcity mindset to the abundance mindset of Jesus."[39] Generosity is both a spiritual discipline and a declaration of trust in God's provision. It is an outward action that reshapes our inward beliefs.

It can be intimidating to give an abundant gift, but the only way to truly discover the joy and fulfillment that comes from generosity is to step into it yourself. Living with an abundance mindset requires practicing generosity in real-time.

Today, I want to show you two examples of amazing women in the Bible who "tried it" and were commended by Jesus Himself. One offered a small gift. Another offered a massive gift.

A SMALL GIFT

The first woman is found in Luke 21:1-4:

> **As Jesus looked up, he saw the rich putting their gifts into the temple treasury. He also saw a poor widow put in two very small copper coins. "Truly I tell you,"** **he said,** **"this poor widow has put in more than all the others. All these people gave their gifts out of their wealth; but she out of her poverty put in all she had to live on."**

The widow's gift was small by worldly standards, yet Jesus declared it the greatest because it came from a heart of complete trust and surrender. While the wealthy gave out of their net worth, she gave out of her lack. This was a radical act of faith.

This story challenges common misconceptions about generosity. Abundant giving is not about the amount but about the heart. Even those with little can live generously when their trust is in God.

Sadly, statistics today reflect a sobering truth: The more people earn, the less they tend to give proportionally. Research from *The State of the Bible 2024* reveals that those earning under $30,000 annually give a higher percentage of their income to charity than those in higher income brackets.[40]

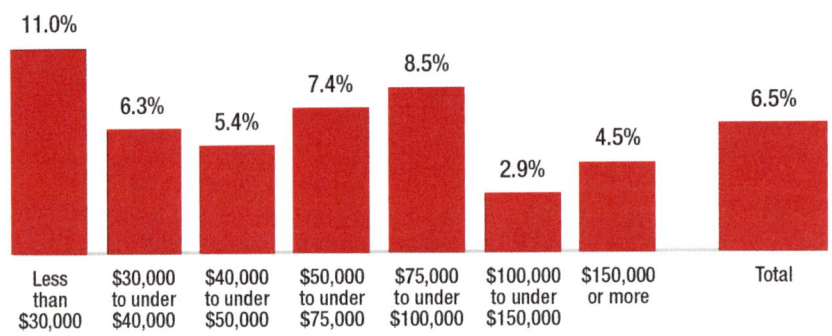

The lie many of us believe is that once I get more, then I'll give more. But the opposite is what's being played out. The more you get, the more you hold onto. Wealth often creates a false sense of security, making it harder to release resources. If you are not generous with a little, you will not turn into a generous person when you have much.

That's why generosity doesn't start at a certain income level. Generosity starts not with wealth but with faith. While the widow's offering came from a place of profound faith, another woman's radical generosity exemplifies a different yet equally powerful expression of the abundance mindset.

A MASSIVE GIFT

The second woman's story is found in Matthew 26:6-13:

> **While Jesus was in Bethany in the home of Simon the Leper, a woman came to him with an alabaster jar of very expensive perfume, which she poured on his head as he was reclining at the table.**
>
> **When the disciples saw this, they were indignant. "Why this waste?" they asked. "This perfume could have been sold at a high price and the money given to the poor."**
>
> **Aware of this, Jesus said to them, "Why are you bothering this woman? She has done a beautiful thing to me. The poor you will always have with you, but you will not always have me. When she poured this perfume on my body, she did it to prepare me for burial. Truly I tell you, wherever this gospel is preached throughout the world, what she has done will also be told, in memory of her."**

This woman poured an entire jar of perfume—worth a year's wages—on Jesus. The disciples criticized her, seeing it as wasteful. Yet Jesus praised her, recognizing both the depth of her devotion and the prophetic significance of her gift.

Her sacrifice was extravagant, but she understood the greatness of who Jesus was. She gave her most valuable possession to Him, foreshadowing the breaking of His body for all of humanity. Her story is a powerful example of the abundance mindset: giving freely, without hesitation, for a purpose far greater than ourselves.

As I've written about in *Serving Challenge*, this woman's abundant gift was likely given on the Wednesday, two days before Jesus's crucifixion. Perfumes and aromas are powerful, especially when an entire jar is poured out. It's likely that, even 48 hours later, the scent still lingered on the body of Jesus as He was breaking it for us.

In this way, you could say that every time we preach about Christ's crucifixion, we also speak of this woman's sacrifice. As a preacher once said, "The only good thing Jesus wore to His crucifixion was the fragrance of this woman."[41]

It's possible that the lovely scent of this woman's abundant sacrifice gave Jesus a small respite in an otherwise brutal six-hour stint where He broke everything for you and for me. I love to think about it that way. When we give abundantly, we mirror the abundant love and grace of Jesus hanging on that cross. We preach the Gospel not just with words but through our actions.

Generosity is not about the size of the gift. Jesus commends two women, one who gave a small amount and one who gave a massive amount. Jesus was less focused on the size of the gift and more on the posture of the heart.

Do you want to live with an abundance mindset? Do you want a heart that reflects God? What's stopping you? Try it.

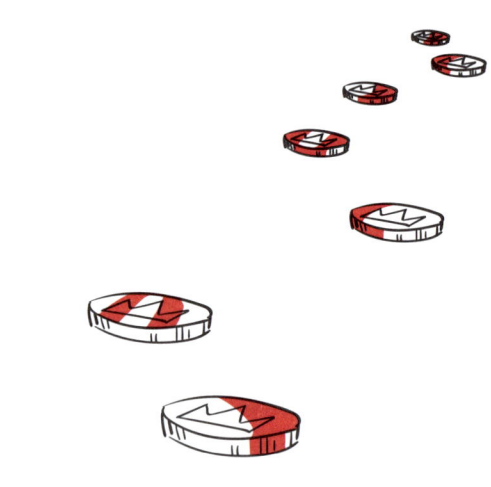

CHALLENGE

WRAP-UP DAY

Today, as we wrap up the Giving Abundantly week, I pray that you feel ridiculously cared for and provided for by Jesus so that you never live with a scarcity mindset again. Spend some time reflecting on your gift and how you can keep trading scarcity for abundance in your life.

If you gave yesterday, how did it feel?

_____

_____

What would it look like to permanently trade a scarcity mindset for an abundance mindset in your life?

_____

_____

What was one major takeaway, feeling, or lesson that you received from this week's devotions and challenges?

_____

_____

26/40

DAYS 27-33

OF THE 40-DAY CHALLENGE

WEEK 5: GIVING REGU

TRADING CONTROL FOR OBEDIENCE

"You cannot serve both God and money."

Matthew 6:24b

DAY 27

MUSTARD-SEED HABITS

> "The kingdom of heaven is like a mustard seed."
> Matthew 13:31b

When it comes to living out your God-given purpose, it's easy to dream about the big picture and the ways God can use you to make a difference. But the reality is this: Purpose isn't just about where you'll end up; it's about the steps you take every day to get there. The habits you build, what you do regularly and faithfully over time, ultimately shape your life and determine whether you'll fulfill the purpose God has uniquely given you.

Think about it this way: Everyone has goals. Goals are important because they give you direction. But you do not live by goals alone. What matters far more are the systems, particularly the habits that you create to achieve those goals. If your goal is to get in shape, establishing the goal itself doesn't make you healthier. What transforms you is the system: waking up early, showing up at the gym, planning healthy meals, and staying consistent.

James Clear, author of *Atomic Habits* says, "You do not rise to the level of your goals. You fall to the level of your systems."[42]

I am a testament to this.

I came into last year with one goal: to write the first draft of *Giving Challenge* by year's end. But here's the truth: If I only had a goal but not a system underneath, I wouldn't have accomplished it.

Eighty-one percent of Americans believe they can write a book, yet only 3 percent actually do. Why? What stops most people is a practical issue: time management. I've coached many aspiring writers, and I always tell them: Writing requires a system of habits. One of the best habits? Time-block your calendar. Schedule writing hours and stick to them.

Writing is just like getting back into the gym. The first reps, those early writing sessions, are tough, especially after a long break. But if you regularly and faithfully keep showing up, the work gets better, the words flow, and you improve. It's all about the reps.

Having a clear purpose or even a goal to attain helps you start with the end in mind, while systems and habits keep you on track and moving in the right direction.

The same is true for your finances. If you want your money to reflect God's purpose for your life, you can't just hope, or even just set a goal, to be generous. You must have a system, or habits, that help you move consistently in this direction.

SMALL STEPS, BIG RESULTS

New research from Duke University shows that over 40 percent of the actions we take every day aren't intentional decisions at all. Instead, they're automatic habits.[43] That research stopped me in my tracks. If nearly half of our lives are spent on autopilot, then we shouldn't be so focused on making better decisions but rather building better habits. Imagine the greater impact we would have if we could eliminate the need to constantly choose the right or wrong direction because we have habits in our lives that automatically point us in the right direction.

This research and thinking are important in our everyday lives, especially in our finances. Too often, if we don't have a system, or some built-in habits, in our lives, if you are anything like me, you will spend money on something and later look back and have regret, or remorse, over your spending decisions.

When it comes to fulfilling our God-given purpose, we often think we need to make giant leaps forward. But more often than not, it's the small, consistent steps, particularly the habits we build, that have the biggest impact over time. Jesus illustrates this beautifully when He says:

> **"The kingdom of heaven is like a mustard seed, which a man took and planted in his field. Though it is the smallest of all seeds, yet when it grows, it is the largest of garden plants and becomes a tree, so that the birds come and perch in its branches." Matthew 13:31b-32**

A mustard seed starts small, almost insignificant. Yet with time and care, it grows into something substantial. The same is true for the systems and habits we build into our lives. A single habit, like faithfully managing your time, your finances, or serving others, might feel small in the moment. But over time, those habits compound, and significant change comes.

As I was writing this book and looking at the different ways in which Jesus gave, if I'm honest with you, I thought this might be the most boring of the weeks. Giving regularly? "Regular" is not a fun word. It's certainly not as fun as words like happy, eternal, and abundant. Yet, it's often in the ordinary, regular moments of life, our everyday habits, where our purpose is either realized or missed.

LONG OBEDIENCE IN THE SAME DIRECTION

Generosity may start small: setting aside a portion of your income, intentional spending, reducing debt, or helping someone in need. Like the mustard seed, those daily choices may not seem like much at first, but they add up.

We live in a microwave society where we want and expect everything fast. But the way the Kingdom of God works is the opposite of this. There is no overnight success when it comes to being a generous person.

Instead, to borrow Eugene Peterson's line, what's most important to becoming the person God is calling you to become is "long obedience in the same direction."

You have likely heard that people often overestimate what they can do in the short-term. But the flip side is true as well. People often underestimate what they can do in the long-term. This week, we will be focusing on getting practical to help you build the habits, or systems, of a generous person into your life so that ultimately you can become the person God has uniquely designed you to be.

God isn't asking us to accomplish everything all at once. He's inviting us to plant the seed, to take the first step, and to trust Him with the growth. If we're obedient in the small things, we trust He will multiply them into something far greater than we could imagine.

So, what small step can you take today? What habit can you begin that aligns with your God-given purpose? Don't underestimate the power of long obedience in the same direction. A mustard seed may look small, but when you partner with God, even the smallest act of faithfulness can grow into something extraordinary.

CHALLENGE

CONTROL OR OBEDIENCE CHECK

Place a checkmark next to the statement that best describes you currently—not who you aspire to be, but how you're living right now.

- ☐ You anticipate negative outcomes if you're not in charge.
- ☐ You trust God to bring about His best outcomes.
- ☐ You want to hoard resources for security.
- ☐ You freely share, trusting God to provide.
- ☐ You don't have regular habits of generosity in your life.
- ☐ You have regular habits of generosity in your life.
- ☐ Your money is not tied to your overall purpose.
- ☐ Your money reflects your overall purpose.
- ☐ If someone looked at your financial accounts, they wouldn't know if you followed Jesus.
- ☐ If someone looked at your financial accounts, they would know you follow Jesus.
- ☐ You do everything you can to make sure things go according to your plan.
- ☐ You trust God's plan even when you don't understand it.
- ☐ You give less than 10 percent of your income to advancing God's kingdom.
- ☐ You give 10 percent or more to advancing God's kingdom.
- ☐ You worry about things going wrong.
- ☐ You rest in God's sovereignty.

#GIVINGCHALLENGE

☐ There is no discernable difference between you and someone who doesn't follow Jesus.	☐ You are discernably different than someone who doesn't follow Jesus.
☐ You give after everything else is paid for.	☐ You give the first opportunity you have.
☐ Your lifestyle continues to get more lavish the more money you make.	☐ Your lifestyle remains consistent no matter how much money you make.
☐ You think more about your net worth than your annual giving.	☐ You think more about your annual giving than your net worth.
☐ You do not deny yourself anything.	☐ You deny yourself of things daily.

Count the number of checkmarks on the right side and circle the number below.

If your number is low, you are likely living with a posture of control with your finances. If your number is high, you are living in obedience to God with your finances.

Control 1 2 3 4 5 6 7 8 9 10 11 12 13 **Obedience to God**

Whatever your number might be, set a goal to improve by at least two or three points. What action or next steps can you take this week to get better? Write it down and act on it.

27/40

DAY 28

WHAT'S YOUR MISSION?

> "My Father, if it is possible, may this cup be taken from me. Yet not as I will, but as you will."
>
> **Matthew 26:39b**

People often take significant time to craft mission statements and visions for their businesses and organizations. Yet, how often do we apply that same effort to clarify the purpose of our personal lives? Have you ever taken a moment to ask yourself, "Why am I here? What is my God-given purpose?"

These are foundational questions, and seeking God's guidance to answer them is vital to living the life you were called to live. Knowing why you live also makes a difference in how you steward your finances.

At the heart of our existence as believers lies a shared macro-purpose: to glorify God. This purpose is woven throughout Scripture and serves as our ultimate destination in all that we do. But within this greater purpose, each of us is given a unique calling—a "micro-purpose" that reflects our individual talents, circumstances, and passions.

When we lack clarity about our purpose, life can feel aimless. Decisions feel scattered, and we may feel like we're just drifting through life. But when we take the time to clarify our God-given purpose, it acts like a compass. It helps us make better decisions and stay focused, especially in complex areas of life like our finances.

THE OBEDIENCE OF JESUS

Jesus's life offers the perfect example of how knowing your purpose can lead to greater clarity. From the moment He began His ministry, Jesus was laser-focused on His mission: to restore humanity's relationship with God through His sacrifice.

Jesus could have chosen a life of wealth, comfort, and power, all things that were well within His grasp. Yet, He chose to let go of the need to control His life and instead to fulfill His higher calling. We see the weight of this calling most clearly in the Garden of Gethsemane. In one of His most human and vulnerable moments, Jesus prayed, **"My Father, if it is possible, may this cup be taken from me. Yet not as I will, but as you will." Matthew 26:39b**

This prayer reminds us that obedience is not always easy. It requires surrender—letting go of your desire to control. Jesus didn't just submit to God's will out of duty. He did so because His purpose—to glorify the Father by redeeming humanity—was deeply ingrained in Him. This purpose gave Him the strength to endure the cross.

Now imagine if Jesus hadn't known His purpose. What if He had succumbed to the temptations of the devil in the wilderness (Matthew 4:1–11) or abandoned His mission when faced with opposition? Without a clear sense of purpose, it's easy to imagine a very different outcome. But because Jesus understood why He was here, He remained obedient, even in the most agonizing moments.

MY GAMBLING STORY

Like Jesus, we are called to align every part of our lives, including our finances, with God's purposes for our lives. Without clarity about your purpose, you can easily fall into the world's patterns of just pursuing more wealth, comfort, and self-interest.

I've experienced this firsthand, especially when I was newly married.

Allison and I got married young. I was just 21, and we each had a semester of college to finish. After graduation from college, I went through a season of waiting. I had close to a nine-month gap between college and seminary. Although I knew I was called to pastoral ministry, I wasn't there yet. At the same time, I started an online business that gave me my first taste of financial freedom. Sadly, because I felt that my true purpose was on hold, I made horrible choices that didn't align with where God was calling me.

Online gambling, a new phenomenon at the time, seemed like a harmless way to pass the time. But it quickly spiraled out of control. I lost $10,000 in just a few months. Hitting rock bottom and confessing my actions to my wife was a wake-up call. I realized that without a clear purpose guiding me, my finances were completely out of alignment with God. And, as my money went, so went my heart with it.

When we don't intentionally define our purpose, the world supplies a path for us to follow, and sadly, I fell for it. I knew where I was headed in life overall, but I wasn't living out my purpose in those months.

The turning point came when I made the decision to once again surrender control of my life, especially my finances, to God. I was entering into ministry, and I knew I could no longer let money control me. I had to stop making financial decisions out of self-interest and greed. Instead, I needed to get help and then align my financial choices with what I was put on earth to do.

To give up control of what I wanted, I needed to hold onto a larger mission. That mission, of course, was to fully surrender to God. Rather than just knowing Jesus as my Savior, I made it my life's calling to serve Him as my Lord. I would be obedient to God's mission. When we release control and choose obedience, we begin to experience the peace that comes from trusting God's plans over our own.

LETTING GO

After haphazardly wasting so much of our money, my wife and I got serious about putting habits into our lives to reflect generosity. And, as our habits of generosity have developed, our hearts for God's Kingdom have grown even more. For 20 years, we've practiced generosity habits, and we have grown in our generosity.

One way that I'm sure I'm on the right track is when I prepare my taxes. At the very end, right before I hit "submit," the tax software performs an audit risk. Every year, one red flag always pops up because my charitable contributions seem excessive compared to the national average. I smile every time I see this because it reminds me how far I've come.

If someone were to look at my financial statements from the past 20 years, they'd be able to tell I'm growing in my pursuit to follow Jesus. I certainly have more room to grow, but someone could easily tell that I am not following the ways of the world when it comes to how my money is being spent.

Part of my reason for writing this book is to complete my own journey of healing from using money improperly. If I can admit my mistake, surrender to God, get help, and help others, honestly, I'm not sure there is anything personally more fulfilling than that!

My story about money says, "If I can change, so can you!"

When you surrender your finances to God and align them with His purpose, it changes everything. Your decisions about money become less about you and more about serving God with what you have.

As you embrace your God-given purpose, your life will shift from aimless drifting to intentional living. Your finances, relationships, and decisions will all come into alignment with something far greater than yourself. The focus will no longer be on yourself but on glorifying God in everything you do.

If you find yourself struggling with your finances, remember this: You have the power to change. It starts with seeking God's guidance and surrendering your control to Him. When you do, you will begin to experience a new level of peace, direction, and freedom. Just like Jesus, you may even at times say something like this: "My Father, not my will, but Yours be done."

Becoming generous isn't always easy, but it is a defining mark of those who follow Jesus. This week, you'll be encouraged to put biblical generosity into practice. By building habits of generosity, you'll keep your life's purpose to glorify God at the center of your life, no matter what challenges or circumstances come your way.

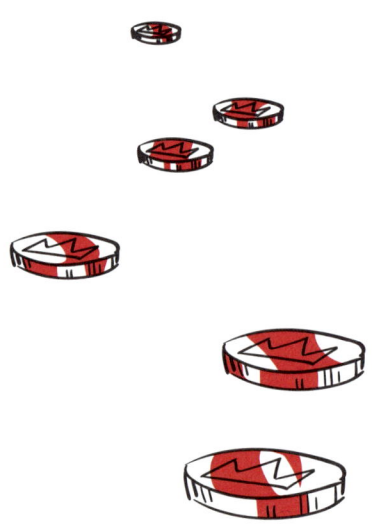

CHALLENGE

LOOK TO JESUS

Read Matthew 26:36-56: How does Jesus's prayer in the Garden of Gethsemane show His willingness to follow God's purpose, even when it was difficult?

What does Jesus's life and mission teach us about trusting God's plans over our own desires?

Why is it significant that Jesus chose to endure the cross rather than seek an easier or more comfortable life?

28/40

DAY 29

TITHING IN THE MOSAIC LAW

> "So give back to Caesar what is Caesar's, and to God what is God's."
>
> **Matthew 22:21b**

One of the habits of giving that gets talked about the most in Christian circles is the tithe.

Tithing, by definition, is the act of giving away 10 percent of your income. Yet, some say, "I tithe 5 percent of my income," but that's a misunderstanding of the word "tithe." A true tithe is intentionally giving one-tenth, or 10 percent, of your income.

This misunderstanding likely contributes to why so many people think they're tithing. Twenty to 40 percent of Christians claim to tithe. But in reality, only about 5 to 10 percent of them give 10 percent or more of their income. Looking at all Americans, only 2 to 4 percent give more than 10 percent of their income.

The math doesn't add up.

In short, tithing is widely discussed but rarely practiced, yet it continues to be taught by some as the gold standard for giving. Over the next few days, I'll challenge that perspective and offer a more biblical, Jesus-centered approach.

One of the most striking aspects of Jesus's teaching on giving comes from His response to a loaded question about taxes: **"So give back to Caesar what is Caesar's, and to God what is God's." Matthew 22:21b** While this statement was aimed at a specific debate about taxes, its implications reach far beyond. It challenges us to consider not just our financial obligations to earthly systems, but our spiritual and practical commitments to God.

When we examine the practice of tithing through this lens, the question becomes: What is God's, and what are we giving back to Him? The truth is, as we've learned already, everything we have belongs to God. The Old Testament tithes were structured to reflect this reality, pushing God's people to live lives of consistent, generous devotion. It wasn't just about fulfilling a law; it was about recognizing God's ultimate ownership and their reliance on His provision.

But is the tithe still relevant today? Since this topic is too expansive for one reading, we'll break it down over several days. Today, we'll explore its biblical roots, particularly in the Mosaic Law, laid out in the first five books of the Old Testament.

The first recorded tithe appears early in Genesis. After a victorious battle, Abraham gave 10 percent of the spoils to Melchizedek, the high priest (Genesis 14:18-24). What's even more remarkable, but less discussed, is that Abraham also gave away the remaining 90 percent to the community. This is the first example of someone fully acknowledging God as the owner of all things, and it happened before the Mosaic Law.

The Mosaic Law outlined God's instructions for the Israelites, including the Ten Commandments, but it went much further. Across Exodus, Numbers, Deuteronomy, and Leviticus, 613 laws detail how an Israelite should live in devotion to God. Many Christians know tithing is taught in the Old Testament commandments, but few realize that many Israelites were instructed to give not one tithe, but three.

If the average Israelite followed the Law to the letter, they would give closer to 23 percent of their income through these three tithes.

THE THREE TITHES

I don't remember learning about three different tithes until researching this book. To be fair, it's possible I was taught this but wasn't paying attention, or it went in one ear and out the other. I've listened to thousands of sermons and can't recall one covering what I'm about to share. And yes, I've read the Bible many times, but these laws in Leviticus, Numbers, and Deuteronomy are easy to gloss over.

If I, a person with a Master of Divinity who has served in pastoral ministry for over 15 years, didn't know about this, chances are you haven't heard it either.

That's why I've included the biblical references for each of the three tithes I'll explain, so you can look them up for yourself. Reading these verses will be part of the daily challenge to complete.

❶ THE LEVITICAL TITHE (NUMBERS 18:20-24)

Israel was divided into 12 tribes, and one of those tribes, the Levites, had a unique role. They served as priests and religious officials for the entire nation. Their duties in the Tabernacle and Temple included leading music, maintaining the facilities, performing ceremonies, and assisting the high priest. This work was their full-time vocation.

Unlike the other tribes, the Levites were not allowed to own land or receive an inheritance. To provide for them, God commanded the Israelites to give a 10-percent annual tithe to support the Levites and their families as they carried out their sacred responsibilities.

Today, the Levitical tithe serves as a model for the tithe we give to the church. Just as the Israelites supported the Levites in their full-time ministry, our giving helps provide for pastors, church staff, and the work of the church. This tithe ensures that those dedicated to teaching, shepherding, and serving the body of Christ can continue their calling without financial burden, allowing them to focus on ministering to God's people.

❷ THE FESTIVAL TITHE (DEUTERONOMY 14:22-27; 26:10-16)

This second tithe funded the Feast of Tabernacles, an annual festival honoring and remembering God's rescue of the Israelites from slavery in Egypt. What makes this tithe unique is that it wasn't given throughout the year. Instead, people collected it and brought it to the festival. Most brought animals, grain, wine, or olive oil, which they would literally "eat" and "drink" as part of the celebration.

Those unable to bring cattle, food, and drink were instructed to sell them locally and use the proceeds, their own silver, to buy what they needed when they got to the festival. Both the festival and the tithe were about bringing the best to celebrate, remember, and revere God. Along with celebrating, participants were reminded not to forget the Levites and the poor in their giving so they too could enjoy the Festival.

Side note: Imagine spending 10 percent of your income every year on a massive party to honor and celebrate how God has saved you!

❸ THE POOR TITHE (DEUTERONOMY 14:28-29)

Israel operated on a seven-year cycle, and this tithe was specifically given in the third and sixth years of that cycle. Collected over a three-year period, the tithe was then distributed to the poor and needy, with special emphasis on foreigners, orphans, and widows.

Certain groups were exempt from some or all tithes. Levites, who gave one tithe to support the high priest, were not required to contribute further. The high priest, without a way to generate income, was also exempt. Similarly, the poor, defined in the Bible as those without land and owning fewer than 10 animals, were likely exempt.

When combined, these three tithes amounted to roughly 23 percent of an Israelite's income, directed toward causes God cared about: providing for those who served in the Temple, honoring His name, and helping those in need.

When you begin to get the full picture, you can see that tithing in the Old Testament was less about giving away 10 percent to fulfill a law; it was more like a *lifestyle* of generosity that allowed His people to be reverent toward God and compassionate toward each other.

But what does this all mean for us today? Does the Old Testament model of tithing still apply? Are we to give 10 percent? Or should we seek to give closer to 23 percent? Is there a deeper, more transformative approach that Jesus calls us to? Let's explore this further tomorrow, as we unpack how tithing fits into the life of a modern believer and how and whether we can live out these biblical principles in our own lives today.

#GIVINGCHALLENGE

CHALLENGE

TRACK YOUR MONEY

Take time to reflect on your current giving habits. Understanding where your generosity stands is the first step toward lining up your finances with God's purpose. To get a clear picture of your giving, record the following specific areas for your last 12 months.

TOTAL GIVING PERCENTAGE

- Calculate the percentage of your total income that you give. Is it 10 percent (a tithe), less, or more? _____

CATEGORIES OF GIVING

Break down your giving into categories, such as:

- **Church or Ministry Support:** Tithes, offerings, or donations to your local church or spiritual leaders _____

- **Helping the Poor and Needy:** Contributions to organizations or individuals in need (e.g., food banks, shelters, or mission work) _____

- **Other Generosity:** Gifts to friends, family, or other causes not categorized above _____

REGULARITY OF GIVING

- Note how often you give: weekly, monthly, annually, or sporadically. Is your giving consistent and intentional, or does it happen only when you feel prompted?

☐ Weekly   ☐ Monthly   ☐ Annually   ☐ Sporadically

HEART BEHIND THE GIVING

- Reflect on your motivation. Are you giving out of obligation, gratitude, worship, or something else? This is key to understanding how your heart aligns with God's purpose for generosity.

☐ Obligation   ☐ Gratitude   ☐ Worship   ☐ Something Else: _____

1 What stands out to you about your current giving habits?
- Were you surprised by your total giving percentage? Do you feel that your giving reflects your priorities and faith, or are there areas where you want to grow?

_____

_____

_____

#GIVINGCHALLENGE

2 What steps can you take to be more intentional and consistent in your giving?
- Do you need to set a giving goal, automate your generosity, or reallocate funds toward causes that align with your values? How can you ensure generosity is a priority in your financial life?

_____

_____

_____

3 What difference are you making for God's Kingdom through your generosity?
- As you reviewed your giving, write about the impact that your generosity has made in the lives of others. How does that make you feel to know that your generosity has helped others?

_____

_____

_____

DAY 30

SPLIT OPINIONS ON TITHING

> "Do not think that I have come to abolish the Law or the Prophets; I have not come to abolish them but to fulfill them."
>
> **Matthew 5:17**

Did you know that the Bible mentions only one instance in which we're invited to test God? It's in Malachi 3, and it has to do with the tithe.

At the time, the Israelites had begun to relax on the command to tithe. But their struggles went deeper than that. They weren't just withholding from God; they were drifting away from Him. They corrupted the sacrificial system, hoarded their wealth, and turned to worship other gods. God, in His passion and holiness, refused to let this continue.

Throughout the book of Malachi, you can hear God's heart calling His people back to faithfulness.

In this context, God delivers a bold challenge:

> "Bring the whole tithe into the storehouse, that there may be food in my house. Test me in this," says the LORD Almighty, "and see if I will not throw open the floodgates of heaven and pour out so much blessing that there will not be room enough to store it." Malachi 3:10

The tithe God refers to is likely the Levitical Tithe. As we learned yesterday, this tithe supported the work of the Levites and the functions of the Temple. Today, this tithe is associated with funding the work and ministry of the church.

The bigger question remains: "Is this passage still relevant for us today?" After all, this passage comes from the Old Testament. So, here's what we need to wrestle with: Does God's challenge still apply to us now, or was the tithe only a requirement for the Israelite people?

SPLIT OPINIONS

To tithe or not to tithe. That is the question. Three common beliefs are taught about tithing today:

1. Some believe Christians are required to tithe.
2. Others argue Christians *should* tithe, even if it's not a strict requirement.
3. Some believe Christians are not obligated to tithe at all.

Pastors are split on this subject. John Cortines and Gregory Baumer, in their book *God and Money*, highlight a survey in 2011 in which pastors and denomination leaders were asked their opinion on the tithe. "The survey found that 42% of respondents believe that giving 10% of one's income is mandatory today, while 58% do not believe it is mandatory."[44]

The split in opinion is why the word "tithe" is never even mentioned in some churches, while in others, it's a part of nearly every worship service.

This divide over tithing points to a bigger question: How do we approach Old Testament laws in light of the New Testament?

UNDER THE LAW OR NOT?

The reason it's so challenging to decide where to land on tithing may come back to what you believe about Old Testament laws. How do we know which laws of the Old Testament still apply today, and how do we know which ones do not?

Jesus gives us a clue about this in Matthew 5:17: **"Do not think that I have come to abolish the Law or the Prophets; I have not come to abolish them but to fulfill them."** Jesus didn't discard the Old Testament. Instead, He fulfilled it, helping to bring its ultimate meaning to light.

First, like Jesus, we must acknowledge that God's Word, from front-to-back, is inspired. 2 Timothy 3:16-17 reminds us of this truth:

> **All Scripture is God-breathed and is useful for teaching, rebuking, correcting and training in righteousness, so that the servant of God may be thoroughly equipped for every good work.**

God gives us the Bible to equip us. As we learn about God, we grow in our faith in Jesus Christ. This then spurs us on to do good works. But you need the whole counsel of God, not just parts of it. The New Testament, through Jesus, fulfills and completes the Old Testament. Sometimes, it seems Christians selectively apply Scripture to fit an agenda. Whenever Christian leaders and pastors do this, it is tragic.

God gives us the story of the Israelites and the Old Testament so we can learn from it. We learn about the promise of Jesus Christ coming into the world to save us from our sins, and we also gain wisdom and knowledge through the experience of our people in the Old Testament. The Bible's message of Jesus Christ crucified and risen for the sake of the world is what the Bible is all about. We also learn from the Bible what it looks like to follow Jesus today.

In the Bible, some teachings are contextual, meaning they were written for a specific time, place, and group of people. This is true not only for the Old Testament laws given to the Israelites, like those found in Leviticus, but also for certain passages in the New Testament.

The challenges faced by the Israelites in the Old Testament and the apostles in the New Testament were unique to their culture and time. For instance, it wouldn't have made sense for God to address issues like smartphones, artificial intelligence, or social media because those didn't exist in their world. However, just because the Bible doesn't specifically mention these things doesn't mean God's wisdom can't guide how we navigate them today.

In the same way, while some Old Testament laws were tied to Israel's context, the principles behind them, like faithfulness, obedience, and generosity, often transcend time. God's call to generosity is consistent throughout Scripture. But how do we determine whether an Old Testament law still applies to us today?

In short, we look to Jesus and the New Testament to guide us. Where practices like the tithe are reaffirmed, we uphold them. Where Scripture is silent, and neither commands nor forbids us, we are free to exercise our Christian liberty.

Tomorrow, we'll explore what Jesus Himself said about tithing and discover what's most important to God.

PRAY DAY

Every week you will be challenged to pray about your giving. As you discern what/how to give each week, you will never be told a specific amount. Our recommendation for you is to bring all these decisions before God through prayer.

Here are the prayer steps we'll be asking you to follow each week:

1. Acknowledge that God is most generous and thank Him for His provision.

2. Ask God how you can be generous this week.

3. Listen for His direction. For specifics on how to hear God's voice, check out this blog: "3 Questions to Help You Know if You Are Hearing God's Voice."

4. Be obedient. When God is leading you to give, follow His lead and trust Him fully.

#GIVINGCHALLENGE

If you need more direction, here's a prayer you can pray this week:

Heavenly Father,

I come before You today with an open heart, asking You to guide me in my giving. You are the Ultimate Provider, and all I have comes from You. I do not want my money to control me. I yield to being obedient to You in my finances. So, Lord, what does obedience look like when it comes to my finances? What would You have me give? What practices of generosity would reflect that I am obediently following You? How can I be sacrificial in my generosity so others can experience Your goodness?

God, I'm quieting my heart and listening for Your direction. Give me discernment to recognize Your voice now and clarity to follow where You lead.

Consider pausing in silence for a minute or two.

Lord, I choose to trust You. I will respond with obedience. I know that You see the bigger picture, that You have my best in mind, and that You will always provide for my needs. Help me to release any fear or hesitation, and to give with a joyful heart. May my giving be an act of worship that draws me closer to Your heart.

In Jesus's name,
Amen.

30/40

DAY 31

THE POINT OF THE TITHE

> "With man this is impossible, but with God all things are possible."
> **Matthew 19:26b**

Have you ever felt like you were doing all the right things but still missing the mark? That's what happens when we focus on outward actions and neglect what truly matters to God: our hearts. Jesus made this abundantly clear in His teachings, especially when addressing the Pharisees and the rich young ruler. These stories reveal that God is far less interested in appearances or rule-following and far more invested in capturing our hearts.

Jesus talked about tithing only once, and it's recorded in both Matthew 23 and Luke 11. In Luke 11:42, He says:

> "Woe to you Pharisees, because you give God a tenth of your mint, rue and all other kinds of garden herbs, but you neglect justice and the love of God. You should have practiced the latter without leaving the former undone."

The Pharisees meticulously followed the Law, even tithing the smallest herbs. But their focus on outward compliance masked a deeper issue: They neglected justice, mercy, and love for God. Jesus wasn't condemning tithing; He affirmed it. Yet in the few red-letter mentions of tithing, it was never the main point.

This passage reveals a profound truth: Following rules without a genuine relationship with God leads to all kinds of evil. For the Pharisees, it resulted in hypocrisy, pride, and idolatry. They were consumed with appearing righteous to others but completely missed the purpose of Jesus's mission.

Jesus reserved His harshest words for self-righteousness because it blinds us to our need for God. The Pharisees had incredible potential to do good, but their obsession with outward righteousness left them spiritually bankrupt. When Jesus called them out, it wasn't just a rebuke. It was an invitation to something greater: a real relationship with God.

THE RICH YOUNG RULER MISSED THE POINT

Another powerful example of Jesus addressing the heart comes in His interaction with the rich young ruler in Matthew 19.

> **Just then a man came up to Jesus and asked, "Teacher, what good thing must I do to get eternal life?" Matthew 19:16**

This question reveals a flawed perspective right off the bat. The man assumed eternal life could be earned by doing something, rather than by receiving what God was offering.

Jesus plays along and responds by listing several commandments.

Commandments fall into two categories: those that focus on our relationship with God and those that focus on our relationship with others. Interestingly, the ones Jesus mentions all pertain to the man's relationship with others, leaving out any that directly address his relationship with God.

> **"'You shall not murder, you shall not commit adultery, you shall not steal, you shall not give false testimony, honor your father and mother,' and 'love your neighbor as yourself.'"**

> **"All these I have kept," the young man said. "What do I still lack?" Matthew 19:18b-20**

On the surface, the young man appeared righteous, fulfilling the outer commandments. But Jesus saw the truth: His heart was tied to wealth. He wanted to appear righteous outwardly but was inwardly enslaved to his possessions.

Then Jesus challenged him:

> **"Sell your possessions and give to the poor, and you will have treasure in heaven. Then come, follow me."**

> **When the young man heard this, he went away sad, because he had great wealth. Matthew 19:21b-22**

The issue wasn't that wealth itself is evil. Instead, the story challenges us to examine our lives. Are there things we prioritize over God? How we use money often reveals our idols. Anything we place above God in our hearts is an idol, and idols always take more from us than they give us in return.

For the rich young ruler, his wealth was likely tied to appearance. He used it to appear righteous. But if wealth becomes an idol, it technically violates and assaults the very first commandment: **"You shall have no other gods before me." Exodus 20:3**

Jesus's invitation to the man was radical yet liberating. By letting go of his wealth, he could have gained something far greater: a relationship with the living God. It's been said that if you get the first commandment right, the others will follow. But it doesn't work in reverse. Outward actions cannot replace a heart fully surrendered to God.

THIS IS THE POINT: DON'T MISS IT

After the man left, Jesus turned to His disciples and said:

> **"Truly I tell you, it is hard for someone who is rich to enter the kingdom of heaven. Again I tell you, it is easier for a camel to go through the eye of a needle than for someone who is rich to enter the kingdom of God."** Matthew 19:23b-24

Jesus wasn't condemning wealth. He was warning that material abundance makes it difficult to rely fully on God. Wealth can more easily lead to self-reliance, pride, and misplaced trust. And if anyone tries to achieve salvation on their own, through their own self-reliance, then perfection is demanded.

> **When the disciples heard this, they were greatly astonished and asked, "Who then can be saved?"**
>
> **Jesus looked at them and said, "With man this is impossible, but with God all things are possible." Matthew 19:25-26**

This is the heart of the Gospel. We cannot save ourselves through good actions or outward righteousness. Perfection is the standard, and only God can meet it. That's why Jesus lived a perfect life on our behalf. Through faith in Him, we are freed from the burden of perfection because His righteousness becomes our own.

What does this mean for practices like tithing? Tithing is a powerful habit and ought to be practiced, but Jesus reminds us that tithing has never been about checking a box or earning favor with God. The Law was never meant to be a checklist; it was always designed to draw us closer to Him. It's less about rules and more about relationships.

When Jesus spoke about tithing to the Pharisees, He placed it in proper context. Tithing, like any act of obedience, should flow from a heart that genuinely loves God. Without this foundation, it risks becoming nothing more than an empty ritual.

Tithing, like attending church, reading the Bible, and praying daily, are all good practices that help spur forward your relationship with God. But none of these are ends in themselves. Neither are the outer issues, like social justice and loving your neighbor, which Jesus affirms. You are not and will never be saved by what you do. Ever. If you attempt to rely on your own actions, you'll find the task is impossible, as the disciples said.

Outward obedience to what Jesus asks of us is good. It's even beautiful. But what's best is that by Jesus's grace and through His righteousness, you get to be in relationship with the God of the Universe. That's the end we seek.

The good news is this: God doesn't ask us to rely on our own strength. Through Jesus, God has made the impossible possible. He has bridged the gap between our imperfection and His perfection. When we place our faith in Him, we receive not only salvation but also the power to live a generous life that reflects His heart.

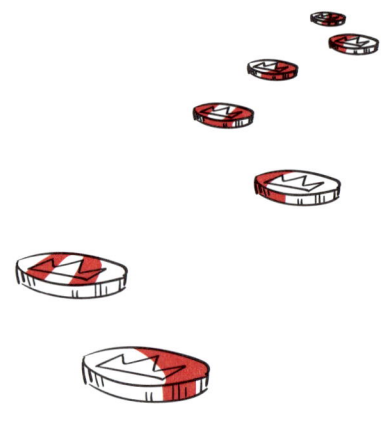

CHALLENGE

PREP DAY

Yesterday you prayed about a gift that you can give away. Tomorrow you will be encouraged to give your gift away.

Write down the gift you are feeling led to give tomorrow. You can write the amount and who you'd like to give the gift to. It can be a person, an organization, or your local church.

AMOUNT: _____

RECIPIENT: _____

As you write your potential gift down, pause and pray. In your prayer, ask God these three questions.

1. Is my gift generous?
2. Is my gift sacrificial?
3. Is my gift obedient?

- If the answers are "yes," then ask God to guide you in staying faithful to your decision.
- If the answers are "maybe," consider if God is asking you to give more.
- If the answers are "no," practice writing a higher number until you feel confident that what you are giving is generous, sacrificial, and obedient.

Let your giving reflect an eternal perspective, knowing that every act of generosity has the power to make a difference for His Kingdom.

31/40

DAY 32

EXCEL IN GIVING

> "Whoever can be trusted with very little can also be trusted with much."
>
> Luke 16:10a

This week, we've explored how habits shape our lives, especially in finances. From clarifying our God-given purpose to creating systems like tithing or cultivating mustard-seed habits, regular generosity is both the expectation and the call for those who follow Jesus. As we wrap up this week focused on building habits of generosity, let me leave you with one final visual: Generosity is not a destination. It is a journey.

When I go on a journey, I want to know not just where I'm headed but how far along I am. That's why I love my Apple Watch. On a four-mile hike with 1,000 feet of elevation gain, it tells me exactly where I am, how much distance remains, and how much more climbing I have to do. It helps me pace myself, adjust when necessary, and stay encouraged as I move toward the goal. And when my watch isn't available, I rely on trail signs to point me in the right direction and tell me how much of the journey is left.

Unlike some other aspects of faith, generosity often has a tangible element. Habits of generosity can serve as markers along our spiritual journey, guiding us and confirming that we're moving in the right direction. While the ultimate focus is on the condition of our hearts rather than achieving specific numbers, the habits we develop and the milestones we reach can show us that our hearts are aligned with God's purpose.

The apostle Paul wrote perhaps the seminal chapters on generosity in the New Testament in 2 Corinthians 8-9. In these chapters, Paul encourages believers to live generously, drawing on the example of the Macedonian church. Although they were poor by all measures, they were so taken by the grace of God that they sought to honor Him with their full selves, including their finances.

Paul uses their example to encourage the Corinthian church to finish a generosity movement they had begun the previous year. He writes:

> **But since you excel in everything—in faith, in speech, in knowledge, in complete earnestness and in the love we have kindled in you—see that you also excel in this grace of giving. 2 Corinthians 8:7**

Paul reminds them that giving is done through grace. It's something for which we should strive to grow and excel.

Generosity doesn't have a final destination. If you have breath in your lungs, you have the opportunity to grow in generosity. You never graduate from it. Wherever you find yourself on the generosity journey, there's always a next step. If lack of generosity is a weakness of yours, get in the game. If you're doing okay, stretch yourself further. If you're already gifted in it, take it to the next level. Jesus is worthy of your best.

Paul also emphasizes intentionality in giving. He writes:

> **Each of you should give what you have decided in your heart to give, not reluctantly or under compulsion, for God loves a cheerful giver. 2 Corinthians 9:7**

Deciding in advance keeps our hearts aligned with God's purposes. Without a plan, we drift into self-serving patterns that prioritize accumulation over generosity. When we go to God, ask, "What does it look like for me to be obedient in my finances?" If we decide in advance how to give, our generosity becomes an act of cheerful surrender and a joyful reflection of His grace.

FAITHFULNESS ALONG THE WAY

A powerful example of this principle comes from the Mizoram church in India. By worldly standards, this church is very poor, much like the Macedonian church in Paul's letter. Although it is poor, this church has developed a habit that is transforming lives far beyond their small community.

The women of the church decided to practice something they call "Buhfai Tham," which translates to "handful of rice." Every time they prepare a meal, they set aside one handful of rice. They gather these small portions throughout the week, and on Sundays, they bring their collected rice to the church, along with their tithes.

Now, you might think, "What difference can a handful of rice make?" But here's the incredible part: The church doesn't just collect the rice. They sell it in the market at a discounted price, ensuring it serves both as an affordable food source for their community and as a means of raising funds.

In 2010 alone, the Mizoram church raised over $1.5 million through this simple habit of generosity. That's right—one handful of rice at a time. And what did they do with this money? They funded missionaries to bring the gospel to the rest of India and the world. Their giving didn't just meet local needs. This small habit is advancing the Kingdom of God.[45]

Imagine that. A community with so little, practicing a habit so small, has had an impact so great. It's a powerful reminder that God doesn't ask us for what we don't have. He invites us to use what He's already given us to bless others and glorify Him.

We look at their story and think it's amazing that they tithe. They are going even beyond the tithe by deciding in advance to use the rice to make a difference in the world.

This reminds us of Jesus's words in Luke 16:10a: **"Whoever can be trusted with very little can also be trusted with much."** The Mizoram church demonstrates that faithfulness with small resources can yield immense blessings. When we steward even the smallest portions well, He entrusts us with more, using our efforts to glorify Him and bless others.

HABITS THAT KEEP YOU ON THE PATH

Your generosity can make a difference, too. Think about the impact you could make with a tithe. It's more than an obligation. It fuels the spreading of the gospel and equips others to grow in faith. The financial support you send to a missionary overseas is a partnership in bringing the message of Jesus to the ends of the earth. The monthly sponsorship of a child in poverty is a tangible expression of God's love for "the least of these."

Even small habits, like giving extra tips for a server or gift cards for the poor, are moments of grace that remind others they are seen, valued, and loved by God.

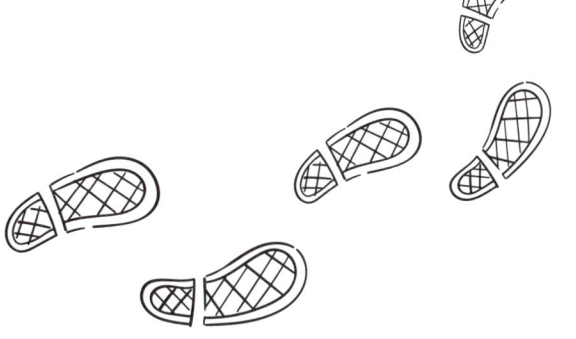

Today, I challenge you to take one bold step toward greater generosity. Maybe it's starting a new habit, like writing down a generosity goal or setting up a recurring gift to your church or a cause you care about. Maybe you've never tithed before, and this is the day when you begin. Maybe your habit is giving the largest amount of money possible to your local church every month. Maybe it's giving sacrificially to someone in need. Whatever it is, let it stretch you. Don't give out of guilt or obligation, but instead give cheerfully, trusting that God will use your gift for His glory and your good.

As we've been teaching you throughout this challenge, ask God: "What does it look like for me to live generously?" Then obey Him. Generosity, at its core, is a response to the grace we've received through Jesus. We were dead in our sins, but Jesus made us alive with Him. Every act of giving is a reminder of what God has already given to us. We can give only because He first gave. So, let us live generously, reflecting His grace to a world in need.

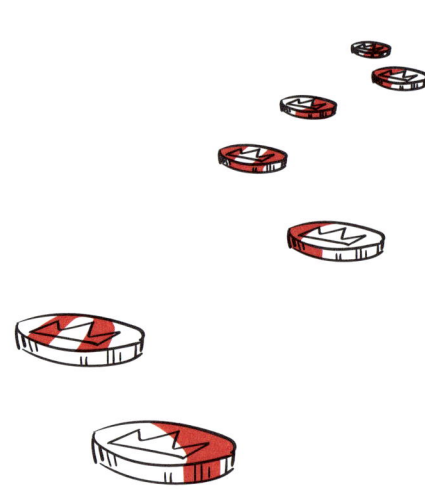

CHALLENGE

GIVE DAY

Today you are being challenged to give your fourth of five gifts during these 40 days. Unlike the previous three gifts, this gift is meant for more than a one-time use, but rather we are challenging you to give this gift regularly or even set up in a recurring fashion. My challenge for you today is to set up this recurring gift for a minimum of six months.

All this week you have studied how Jesus gave regularly to you. You have assessed your current giving habits and seen where you could trade control for obedience. After praying about what God wants you to give this week, be obedient to His call.

Your monetary gift, followed by setting up a recurring or regular gift of generosity in obedience today, will truly help you become the generous person God has called you to be.

DAY 33
LIVING IN THE GRAY

> "Ask and it will be given to you . . . for everyone who asks receives."
>
> **Matthew 7:7a-8a**

Sometimes I wish the Bible was a little more black and white, especially when it comes to generosity. Wouldn't it be simpler if Jesus said, "This is what you should give"? But the Bible doesn't lay it out that way, leaving us to discuss, debate, and discern what generosity looks like for followers of Jesus.

For centuries, tithing has been debated. It was a clear standard in the Old Testament and affirmed by Jesus, although not the main point of His teaching. The apostle Paul emphasizes generosity but doesn't specify percentages. As a result, there's no universal agreement on what giving should look like today. Instead of black and white, we find ourselves in the gray.

Here's the reality: No matter your stance on tithing, actions speak louder than words. As mentioned earlier, only 5 to 10 percent of Christians tithe, and only 2 to 4 percent of American Christians give away 10 percent of their income. Those statistics and others point to little discernible difference in generosity between believers and non-believers. On average, American Christians give away just 2.5 percent of their income. That's it.

Let me be honest. This isn't just sad; it's pathetic. And it's time for a change. Not because generosity is a box to check, but because our lack of generosity reveals a deeper issue. We're called to represent Jesus, and frankly, we've failed. Here's the thing: If we were ignoring Jesus's call and still finding fulfillment, perhaps there'd be an argument for the non-generous life. But even that's not happening. We're missing both the call and the joy that comes with it.

You might wonder why I sound harsh today. "Why the tone? Why the criticism?" Let me answer as a pastor. I've seen this story played out too many times.

I've sat with people who are financially blessed yet feel empty. I've counseled couples making great incomes who list finances as their number one stress. I've watched families earning six figures live paycheck to paycheck. I've seen the world push unattainable financial standards, encouraging people to buy more than they need, only to find themselves drowning in debt. Young people set up lifestyles they can't afford because they're trying to match what their parents built over decades. And the comparison trap, whether it's with flashy neighbors or social media highlight reels, is robbing people of contentment and joy.

It's exhausting. It's sad. And it's frustrating to see people blessed with so much, yet feeling like they lack because they're chasing the world's standards. We need a new relationship with money.

Living by the world's financial expectations is an empty pursuit. It's time to take a stand, to say enough is enough. It's time to put our resources into God's work and get out of this financial, mental, and emotional rut.

For years, some of you have chased a happiness that the world has offered. And what did you get from that? My challenge for you this week is to get into regular habits of generosity. Try six months of being over-the-top generous and see if you are happier. What can it hurt?

The key to a fulfilling life isn't in accumulating more. It's in a real relationship with God. If He has your money, He has your heart. And for many, money is the last thing they surrender to God. This is why so many Christians live half-hearted lives of faith.

Martin Luther once said, "There are three conversions necessary: the heart, the mind, and the purse." Many of you believe in God and are grateful for what He's done, but money holds you back. The world says a good life comes from getting more—more wealth, possessions, and status. But that's a lie, and you've been controlled by it for far too long. True life comes when you let go and trust God completely. Obedience leads to freedom and joy.

IN THE GRAY BUT UNDER GRACE

Here's where I'm torn on tithing. On one hand, if every Christian gave 10 percent, we could eliminate so many of the world's injustices. Just imagine what could be accomplished. Part of me wants to say, "Let's all just hit that mark." But as I've studied Jesus's teachings and lived this out, I know it's not that simple. Tithing as a rule can make us mere box-checkers, missing the relational aspect of generosity. Plus, for some of you, stopping at 10 percent would keep you from experiencing the full joy of giving.

If you're middle-to-upper class, is 10 percent actually generous? I'd argue it's not. Many reading this live in the top 1 percent of global wealth. That gives you two unique opportunities: first, to take greater responsibility for how you steward God's resources, and second, to experience the joy of giving extraordinary amounts to make the biggest difference you possibly can.

For those who like to stick to Old Testament laws, remember that the Israelites gave closer to 23 percent of their income through three tithes, not just 10 percent. If you're playing the Old Testament card, the standard is much higher.

Others argue that, under grace, we're no longer bound to the tithe and can give as we feel led. I agree. But here's the thing: Grace should raise the bar, not lower it. Jesus never lowered the standard. He always raised it. In his book *Money, Possessions, and Eternity*, Randy Alcorn calls tithing the "training wheels of giving." It's a good starting point, but it's not the finish line.[46]

If God were to assess the collective generosity of American believers, the problem wouldn't be that we're giving too much but far too little. In our freedom under grace, we've let the world's pursuit of "more" enslave us. It's time to break free. As God entrusts us with more, our giving should reflect that increase.

To this end, I've created an appendix with 15 generosity habits that can go above and beyond giving a tithe. These habits range from very small (generous tips to your server) to very large (reviewing your estate planning), but all of them are meant to stretch your generosity to look more like Jesus's generosity. They also are opportunities to help you review your regular generosity so that you don't develop a "set it and forget it" mentality when it comes to being generous.

ASK AND BE OBEDIENT

Hopefully, you've learned this week that generosity doesn't happen through random, haphazard giving. Habits matter. Practices like tithing provide a good starting point, but generosity goes beyond hitting a percentage. It's about giving as Jesus did: sacrificially, joyfully, and abundantly.

While having targets in our faith is helpful, following Jesus isn't about adhering to a formula. Tithing is a great place to begin, but for many, it's just the start.

While the Bible does not give you black-and-white rules about generosity, it does give you red letters to help you live in the gray.

In the words of Jesus for today, you are reminded that you are in a real relationship with a living and loving God. When you need anything, especially wisdom or guidance, you have His promise that He will give it to you.

This isn't about guilt or obligation. It's about experiencing the freedom and joy that come from trusting God with everything.

When you give generously, you're declaring that your money doesn't control you. God does. And in that obedience, you'll find a life of impact and fulfillment. So, when it comes to generosity, ask God: What does it look like for me to be generous? And then be obedient to His answer. Trust Him enough to let go of control and give freely.

As you practice obedience, you'll discover what it means to live a generous life. Not only will you reflect the heart of Jesus, but you'll experience the joy, purpose, and impact you were made for.

#GIVINGCHALLENGE

CHALLENGE

WRAP-UP DAY

Today, as we wrap up the Giving Regularly week, I pray that you stepped into a generosity habit that will help you experience God's fulfillment regularly in your life. Spend some time reflecting on the gift you not only gave, but committed to continue to give. Also, reflect on how to trade controlling your own life for being obedient to whatever God asks of you.

If you gave yesterday, how did it feel?

What would it look like to permanently trade control for obedience in your life?

What was one major takeaway, feeling, or lesson that you received from this week's devotions and challenges?

DAYS
34_40
OF THE 40-DAY CHALLENGE

WEEK 6:
GIVING

TRADING GRASPING FOR GRATITUDE

"What good is it for someone to gain the whole world, yet forfeit their soul?"

Luke 14:27

TODAY

DAY 34

DAILY BREAD

> "Give us today our daily bread."
>
> Matthew 6:11

The Lord's Prayer, found in Matthew 6, is the single most-prayed prayer in the history of the world. After acknowledging who God is and then pleading for His Kingdom to come in this world, the first request that we ask of God is to give something to us.

> "Give us today our daily bread."

Have you ever noticed in this request that it's a double, redundant, daily request? It asks for bread "today" and "daily." I wonder if there's not something more to that.

If you are like me, you like to fill your cupboards, cabinets, pantries, closets, garages, and bank accounts to the max. For many of us, this request for God to daily give and daily provide for us feels like a nice thing to say, but we don't actually want to set up our lives to be in daily dependence on God's provision. We often prefer a safety net of comfort, managing resources ourselves rather than depending on God to daily provide.

The idea that God gives daily to not only meet our needs but exceed them is laced all throughout Scripture. Let's look at one of those prime examples from the Old Testament.

When God freed the Israelites from Egypt, they quickly ran out of provisions. Due to their lack of faith in God's promises, they wandered the wilderness for 40 years. With an estimated 2.5 million people, there was no natural way to sustain them.

THE QUAIL MIRACLE

So, God performed the supernatural. For six days each week, He provided manna for the Israelites to eat; and on the sixth day, He gave double the amount so they could gather enough and still observe the Sabbath on the seventh day. This daily dependence on God allowed them to live with and practice contentment.

Each day, they witnessed a miracle. Yet, despite God's faithfulness, they complained about how God was providing for them. They grumbled that there was no meat to eat. To be fair, eating the same thing for 40 years might lead you and me to complain as well. When Allison tried to introduce a "Meatless Monday" into our family, you'd have thought the world was ending. The kids protested like they were being deprived of oxygen, and even I found myself sneaking glances at the fridge, wondering if a quick snack of leftover chicken would go unnoticed.

Despite the Israelites' complaints, God responded in an unexpected way. He provided quail in overwhelming abundance.

Mark Batterson, in *The Circle Maker*, recounts the story from Numbers 11, describing how God provided enough quail to cover the camp about three feet deep and stretch as far as a day's walk. Imagine the scene! This enormous supply was enough to feed the Israelites for an entire month, far beyond what they could have imagined.[47]

This was God showing off and being generous for His people. And, amazingly, it came amid complaining and grumbling, not gratitude. I imagine God saying, "You want meat? I'll give you meat!"

So, if God provided for His people in this way, don't you think He'll still provide for you today?

HE WILL TAKE CARE OF YOU

When Jesus walked this Earth, He continued to remind us of this truth. Perhaps He was never clearer about it than when He issued the words found in the middle of the Sermon on the Mount, which by the way, happens to fall in the exact same chapter as the Lord's Prayer.

You read some of these verses earlier in the challenge. Read them again today, found in Matthew 6:25-30:

> "Therefore I tell you, do not worry about your life, what you will eat or drink; or about your body, what you will wear. Is not life more than food, and the body more than clothes? Look at the birds of the air; they do not sow or reap or store away in barns, and yet your heavenly Father feeds them. Are you not much more valuable than they? Can any one of you by worrying add a single hour to your life?
>
> "And why do you worry about clothes? See how the flowers of the field grow. They do not labor or spin. Yet I tell you that not even Solomon in all his splendor was dressed like one of these. If that is how God clothes the grass of the field, which is here today and tomorrow is thrown into the fire, will he not much more clothe you—you of little faith?"

God is the Ultimate Provider. You and I are His prized possessions. His ultimate treasure. Jesus reminds us of how good He is to birds, flowers, and grass. And, if He is that good to them, of course He will take care of you and me. Jesus's words doubled down on what God was doing in the Old Testament, and if you then add the apostle Paul's words, you are left with the ultimate trifecta:

#GIVINGCHALLENGE

My God will meet all your needs according to the riches of his glory in Christ Jesus. Philippians 4:19

So, what does it come down to? Jesus makes it very clear that the way we treat and even think about our resources and finances is a faith issue. He claims that those of us who constantly worry about His daily provision have little faith.

Rather than grasping for more and more of this world, God invites us to a life of gratitude. The reality is that many of us are living with incredible financial blessing compared to the rest of the world. When you take a step back and remember all that God has given you, how can you not be grateful?

Gratitude comes when you remember that God will provide everything you need. The beautiful part about our God is that in His provision, like with the quail, He will often give us even far more than we need.

When I remember God's provision in my past, it helps me to live with more faith today. And greater faith today will lead me to greater gratitude in my future.

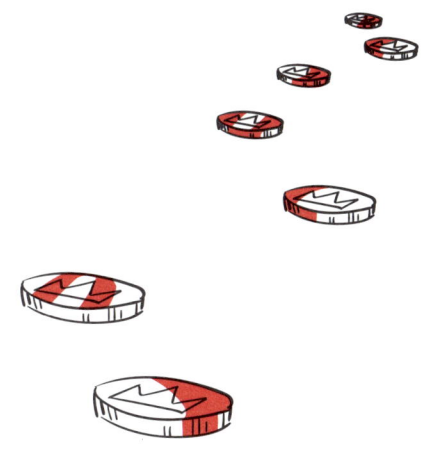

CHALLENGE

GREED OR GRATITUDE CHECK

Place a checkmark next to the statement that best describes you currently—not who you aspire to be, but how you're living right now.

- ☐ You constantly think about how to make more money.
- ☐ You long for more.
- ☐ You spend most of your time thinking of how to better your life.
- ☐ You will give if you get something in return.
- ☐ You try to win at all costs even if it means hurting others.
- ☐ You are jealous when you see what others have.
- ☐ You can't rest until you have achieved more.
- ☐ You are filled with anxiety and stress in your finances.

- ☐ You are thankful for the resources you have to meet your needs.
- ☐ You are grateful for what you have.
- ☐ You spend most of your time thinking of how to help others.
- ☐ You will give because you've already been given much.
- ☐ You are thankful for opportunities to collaborate and grow with others.
- ☐ You celebrate when good things happen to others.
- ☐ You find it easy to rest in the blessings God has provided.
- ☐ You remember daily how God has provided for you.

#GIVINGCHALLENGE

☐	You constantly want to upgrade your lifestyle in some way, shape, or form.	☐	You set limits on your lifestyle.
☐	You don't easily let go of the money that you have.	☐	You live each day open-handed, ready to give as the opportunities arise.
☐	You spend more money than you make.	☐	You make more money than you spend.
☐	You end up having regret or buyer's remorse over things you have bought.	☐	You have no regrets about how you have spent your money.
☐	You make impulsive purchases often.	☐	You deny yourself of things often.

Count the number of checkmarks on the right side and circle the number below.

If your number is low, you are likely living with a mindset of greed. If your number is high, you are living with a heart of gratitude.

Greed 1 2 3 4 5 6 7 8 9 10 11 12 13 **Gratitude**

Whatever your number might be, set a goal to improve by at least two or three points. What action or next steps can you take this week to get better? Write it down and act on it.

34/40

DAY 35

DRACHMA DRAMA

> "Go to the lake and throw out your line. Take the first fish you catch; open its mouth and you will find a four-drachma coin. Take it and give it to them for my tax and yours."
>
> **Matthew 17:27b**

There was a time when Jesus made money appear. Out of nowhere. Grasping the truth of this story will transform how you approach money every single day.

So, let's dive in.

> **When they came to Capernaum, the collectors of the two-drachma tax went up to Peter and said, "Does your teacher not pay the tax?" He said, "Yes." Matthew 17:24-25a (ESV)**

The story starts like so many others involving Jesus: His enemies try to trap Him. Likely, these were Jewish religious officials, people who enjoyed scheming against Him. They corner Peter with a tricky, loaded question.

Don't you love how negative their question is? "Does your teacher not pay the tax?" That's a classic trap. Negative phrasing forces you to overthink. If my wife asked me, "Do you love me?" I'd easily say, "Of course!" But if she asked, "Do you not love me?" I'd pause. Wait, does she think I've done something wrong? To answer, I'd have to counter the negative: "No, I don't *not* love you." See how messy that gets?

That's what's happening here. The tax collectors are setting up Peter with their question. They're not just curious. They're fishing for trouble, and they want Peter to play along.

So, what does Peter do? He says, "Yes." He tells them that Jesus does pay the tax. Except . . . there's a little problem here. Peter straight-up lied.

JESUS STEPS INTO THE MESS

Here's what happens next:

> **And when he came into the house, Jesus spoke to him first, saying, "What do you think, Simon? From whom do kings of the earth take toll or tax? From their sons or from others?" And when he said, "From others," Jesus said to him, "Then the sons are free." Matthew 17:25b-26 (ESV)**

I love this. Before Peter can say a word, Jesus steps in. He knows Peter lied and probably feels conflicted. While Peter's intentions were good—he wanted to protect Jesus—he still lied. How often do we do this? How often do we think we need to defend God, even if it means bending the truth? But here's the thing: God doesn't need us to lie for Him. He doesn't need us to protect Him.

What's beautiful is that Jesus doesn't let Peter sit in his mistake. He steps right into the mess to bring correction. That's what Jesus does. He steps into our conflicts, our bad decisions, and even our messy theology. Not to shame us, but to lovingly set us straight.

JESUS IS TAX EXEMPT

Here's where it gets fascinating. Jesus explains why He doesn't actually owe this tax. To understand this, we need a quick history lesson.

In Exodus 30, God gave Moses instructions for the people of Israel:

> **The Lord said to Moses, "When you take the census of the people of Israel, then each shall give a ransom for his life to the Lord when you number them, that there be no plague among them . . . Everyone who is numbered in the census, from twenty years old and upward, shall give the Lord's offering. The rich shall not give more, and the poor shall not give less, than the half shekel . . . You shall take the atonement money from the people of Israel and shall give it for the service of the tent of meeting, that it may bring the people of Israel to remembrance before the Lord, so as to make atonement for your lives." Exodus 30:11-12, 14-15a, 16 (ESV)**

This tax for all Israelites had two purposes:

1 TO MAKE ATONEMENT FOR SINS.

2 TO SUPPORT THE MINISTRY AT THE TABERNACLE.

Fast forward to Jesus's time. The Tabernacle had become the Temple in Jerusalem, and the half-shekel tax was now two drachma in their currency. But this wasn't a Roman tax; it was a Jewish one, meant to fund Temple upkeep and atone for sins.

Also, there's a problem. The Temple no longer fulfilled its purpose. Jesus called it a "den of robbers," exposing its corruption. He also referred to Himself as the True Temple, saying it would be destroyed and raised in three days—a clear reference to His death and resurrection.

And for atonement? Hebrews explains that Jesus is not a temporary sacrifice but the ultimate one, covering the sins of all people.

So, Jesus asks Peter: Do kings tax their own sons? Of course not. And who is Jesus? The Son of God. He doesn't owe this tax because:

- He is the Temple.
- He is the atonement for sins.

Jesus is exempt. And by extension, so are all who belong to the King's family.

Jesus could have stopped there, telling Peter, "We're not paying, and here's why." But He didn't. Instead, He said:

> **"However, not to give offense to them, go to the sea and cast a hook and take the first fish that comes up, and when you open its mouth you will find a shekel. Take that and give it to them for me and for yourself."**
> **Matthew 17:27 (ESV)**

Amazing, right? Jesus didn't owe the tax. Technically, Peter didn't either. But to avoid unnecessary conflict, Jesus provides a miraculous solution. He tells Peter to go fishing, promising that the first fish he catches will have a shekel in its mouth, which converts to four drachma, the exact amount needed to pay for both of them.

Think about that. Out of thousands of fish in the Sea of Galilee, Jesus directs Peter to the one with the exact coin they need. That's not just a miracle. It's a reminder of who Jesus is. He also allowed Peter to contribute by using his talents. Jesus could've created a coin out of thin air, flipped it to Peter, and said, "Go, give this to them." But much like the feeding of the 5000, which we read about on Day 24, He allowed human beings to contribute to His miracles to feel a deeper connection to Him.

MORE THAN FISH AND CHIPS

Jesus is helping Peter see the bigger picture. At this moment, there are bigger fish to fry. Don't get distracted by the ways of this world.

This story is not about taxes. It's not about the IRS or fish and chips. It's about the Gospel.

Peter had a debt he couldn't pay, and what did Jesus do? He paid it. A man who owed nothing covered the debt of someone who couldn't afford it. Sound familiar?

That's exactly what Jesus has done for you. Every one of us owes a debt to God that we could never pay. But Jesus, the only person who owed nothing, stepped in and paid it. Not with a coin from a fish, but with His own life.

Just like what Jesus did with Peter, He has done the same for you. This story paints a picture of the Gospel: the spotless Lamb of God taking on our sin, paying the price we owed, and setting us free.

When you grasp the depth of Jesus's love and sacrifice, it changes how you approach each day. Your response isn't begrudging obedience or forced good works. Instead, you live in the overflow of gratitude.

When we truly understand what Jesus has done, we can't help but share it with others. We're called to help people out of their debt—not just financial burdens but the spiritual weight they carry. We stop getting sidetracked by the enemy's traps and focus on what truly matters.

This story also reminds us of God's provision. Jesus didn't just pay the debt. He did it in a miraculous, over-the-top way. He didn't need to use a fish, but He did. Why? To show Peter, and us, that He controls everything. The same God who directed that fish to Peter's hook is the God who provides for you today.

He got you off the hook. Now, let's cast our nets for others, trusting that the God of the Universe, who can place a coin in the mouth of a fish, is right there in the boat with you.

#GIVINGCHALLENGE

CHALLENGE

LOOK TO JESUS

Reread Matthew 17:24-27. Why do you think Jesus, who didn't owe the Temple tax, chose to pay it anyway? What does this show about His approach to avoiding unnecessary conflict and focusing on His mission?

___

___

___

How does Jesus's miracle of providing the exact coin through the fish reveal His power and care for both Peter's needs and God's mission?

___

___

___

In this story, Jesus paid a debt Peter couldn't afford to pay himself. Is there a time that God wonderfully provided for you? Describe it here.

___

___

___

35/40

DAY 36

GREED IS SELFISHNESS

> "Watch out! Be on your guard against all kinds of greed."
> Luke 12:15b

Are you greedy? Could you even recognize it if you were?

In the movie *Wall Street*, Michael Douglas's character, Gordon Gekko, famously declares:

> "The point is, ladies and gentlemen, that greed, for lack of a better word, is good. Greed is right, greed works. Greed clarifies, cuts through, and captures the essence of the evolutionary spirit. Greed, in all of its forms—greed for life, for money, for love, for knowledge—has marked the upward surge of mankind. And greed, you mark my words, will not only save Teldar Paper [his company], but that other malfunctioning corporation called the USA."[48]

Douglas won an Academy Award and a Golden Globe for this role. But as you read his words, do you partly believe them? Do you celebrate how your own greed has brought you success?

If so, you'd find yourself at odds with Jesus. He says, bluntly:

> "Watch out! Be on your guard against all kinds of greed." Luke 12:15b

In this quick yet powerful command, Jesus doesn't mince words. He presents two postures for addressing greed: offense and defense. First, He says, "watch out"—be proactive in identifying where greed is at work in your life and the world. Second, He says to "guard against it"—a defensive move to resist its hold once you've recognized it.

These are not casual suggestions. In the original Greek, both phrases are imperatives. Jesus treats greed as a serious, insidious force that demands constant vigilance and action to overcome.

Let's take a closer look at these two postures and how they might play out in your life.

PLAYING OFFENSE AGAINST GREED

Are you watching for greed in your own life? I suspect most of us aren't.

As a pastor, I've been invited into countless moments of confession, where people lay bare their sins and seek absolution. Over the years, I've heard confessions of anger, dishonesty, lust—you name it. But do you know what I've never heard anyone confess? Greed.

It is so easy for this sin to escalate without us even realizing it.

Mary Oliver captures this human tendency beautifully in her poem *I Own a House*:

> "I own a house, small but comfortable. In it is a bed, a desk, a kitchen, a closet, a telephone. And so forth—you know how it is: things collect."[49]

Boy, do they ever.

Consider this: At the founding of the United States, the average American owned just three outfits. Walk-in closets didn't exist. Martha Jefferson, Thomas Jefferson's wife, had 17 outfits, which at the time was considered scandalous.

Today, the average American buys 37 new items of clothing per year and owns about 107. But here's the kicker: Studies show we wear only 10 percent of them. The rest? Twenty-one percent are deemed unwearable, 50 percent don't fit, and 12 percent have never been worn. Despite these overflowing closets, many of us stand in front of them and lament, "I have nothing to wear."

And what about what we throw away? The EPA estimates that each of us discards 68 pounds of clothing and textiles per year.

It's not just clothing, though. The size of the average American home has grown 75 percent over the last century. And yet, the self-storage industry, a business designed to house the things we can't even fit in our ever-larger homes, is booming. There are now more self-storage units in America than McDonald's, Starbucks, Walmart, Target, Taco Bell, and Burger King combined.[50]

If that doesn't make you pause, consider this: Greed may be at the root of nearly every problem that keeps us from living a godly life.

GREED: A DEEPER ROOT THAN YOU THINK

The original sin in the Garden of Eden is often labeled pride. But could greed have been lurking there too? Adam and Eve had everything they needed, yet their desire for more, specifically a fruit that God had expressly forbidden, led them to act. Greed disguises itself in many forms, making it all the more dangerous.

Jemar Tisby, a historian and lifelong racial justice advocate, once connected greed to a different sin: racism. In an interview on my podcast, I asked him, "How did racism begin? What is underneath this egregious sin?" His response shocked me. He said, simply, "Greed."

If he hadn't mentioned this, I never would have connected the dots. I didn't see it. But the more I've reflected, the more I've come to agree. He would go on to say that with so much of the injustices of our world, "the root determines the fruit."[51] Greed, whether for land, power, or wealth, is the root of some of history's darkest chapters. And it continues to drive countless injustices today.

Greed isn't just a personal issue; it's a societal one. And if we celebrate, tolerate, or remain blind to it, we'll drift further from God's desires for us.

PLAYING DEFENSE AGAINST GREED

So, how do we guard against greed?

First, we need to expose the lie that greed is good or that it brings happiness. As we've seen throughout this book, more doesn't equal better. Studies consistently show that chasing "more" will often get you "more." But it won't get you more satisfaction. It'll get you more stress. Greed is different from other desires because it's never satisfied.

Think about it. When you eat, you eventually feel full and stop. When you drink, there's a limit to how much you can consume. But when it comes to accumulating stuff, there's no natural stopping point. And with today's advertising and algorithms working overtime to convince us we need more, the chase for "enough" becomes endless.

The solution? Limits.

Most of us lack limits when it comes to consumption. Without them, we fall into the trap of comparison, collecting more simply because that's what everyone around us seems to be doing. Living without limits doesn't make us freer. It makes us slaves to greed.

Paradoxically, setting limits can help us experience the abundant life Jesus promised. When we stop chasing after "more," we free ourselves to depend on God for our happiness. We learn gratitude, a skill that brings peace and joy in a way greed never could.

GRATITUDE: THE ANTIDOTE TO GREED

Ultimately, gratitude is what allows us to live with limits. It shifts our focus from what we lack to what we've been given. When we cultivate gratitude, we stop seeing limits as restrictions and start seeing them as blessings that protect us from the emptiness of greed.

God has already provided everything we need for what matters most. If we don't define what "enough" looks like for us, greed will define it for us, and it will never be satisfied.

#GIVINGCHALLENGE

Greed is subtle. It hides in plain sight, masquerading as ambition or entitlement. It tells us that the next promotion, the next gadget, the next sale will finally bring fulfillment. But Jesus warns us otherwise.

This isn't a casual warning. It's a call to action. Will you play offense and defense against greed? Will you watch out for greed in your life? Will you guard against it by setting limits and practicing gratitude?

The choice is yours. But one thing is clear: The abundant life Jesus offers can't coexist with unchecked greed.

So, watch out. Guard against it. And remember, God has already given you more than enough.

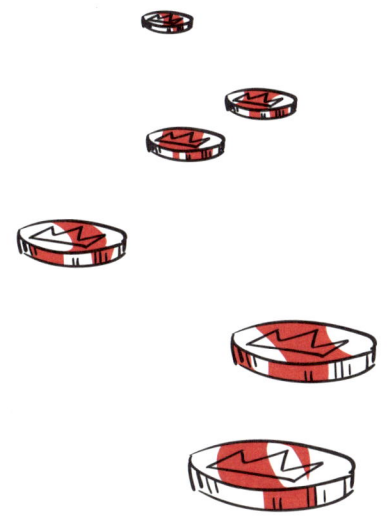

CHALLENGE

TRACK YOUR MONEY

One way to assess greed, both on the defensive and the offensive side, is to watch out for too much debt and too much savings. Too much debt may reveal greed because we don't know how to control our finances. Too much savings may reveal greed because we are focused too much on the things of this world for our security and comfort rather than God.

Today, as you begin to assess your current debts vs. your current savings, you may notice an area for improvement that will help you live more generously each and every day. Total all of your current debts and current savings. Then reflect on how these overall numbers reflect your current heart posture towards money.

DEBTS

Student Loans

Mortgage

Credit Cards

Car Loan

Lines of Credit

Personal Loans

Medical Debt

Other

TOTAL _____

SAVINGS

Bank Accounts

Savings Accounts

Stocks

Retirement Accounts

Money Market Accounts

CDs

Emergency Fund

Other

TOTAL _____

#GIVINGCHALLENGE

1 What does the balance between your debts and savings reveal about your relationship with money?

- Do you find yourself leaning more toward accumulating wealth for security, or do you struggle with managing debt due to lifestyle choices? How does this align with your faith and trust in God's provision?

_____

_____

2 How does your financial posture impact your ability to be generous?

- Does your debt prevent you from giving as freely as you would like? Does your focus on savings cause you to hesitate in sharing with others? What changes could help you live more open-handedly?

_____

_____

3 What practical steps can you take to steward your finances in a way that honors God?

- Do you need to create a plan to reduce debt, set limits on excessive saving, or increase your giving? How can you shift your mindset from financial control to faithful stewardship?

_____

_____

DAY 37

GIVING WITH NO REGRETS

> "Give, and it will be given to you. A good measure, pressed down, shaken together and running over, will be poured into your lap."
>
> **Luke 6:38a**

I was one of the early adopters of GPS technology. Before it was on our phones, I had a Garmin and couldn't wait to show it off, especially to my future father-in-law. Like many in his generation, he was skeptical of this "newfangled" technology.

On vacation one day, we decided to visit a local renowned popcorn shop to grab snacks for the family. I typed the address into my GPS, hit the buttons, and off we went. I followed it faithfully until, drumroll, please . . . we ended up in the middle of a random neighborhood. Nowhere close to the popcorn shop. Fail.

Sometimes the best of the world's directions can lead us to the wrong destination.

But here's the thing: For every time the GPS has led me astray, it has helped me get back on track far more often. When you miss a turn, the GPS doesn't panic. It doesn't criticize or guilt you. Instead, it recalibrates, offering you a new route to get you where you're meant to go. How much more do we need that same kind of recalibration in our lives?

Recalibrating isn't about beating yourself up for missing a turn. It's about refocusing on where you're headed and adjusting your path to get there. And while this principle applies in many areas of life, it's especially important when it comes to how we use our money.

ONE KEY QUESTION

If you're anything like me, you're making money decisions every single day. But without a clear sense of where your life is headed—the final destination—it's hard to know if you are making thoughtful, intentional financial choices in the moment. When you don't have a clear sense of direction, the world is quick to step in and pull you toward its priorities.

For many of us, chasing after worldly things didn't start intentionally. It happened accidentally. We drifted into it because we didn't take the time to calibrate where our lives are today, syncing it with our final destination. Before you know it, you're off the path from where God had intended you to be.

The great news is that when we run into Jesus, we get a chance for a new calibration. Jesus's grace offers us the opportunity of a lifetime: to follow Him daily. When we start seeing each day as following Jesus to the best of our ability as our final and best destination, we begin to view every decision, even our financial choices, with more clarity.

Without that perspective, regret often follows. And that's heartbreaking, because God didn't design us to live stuck in the past. Regret holds us back, but His grace allows us to keep moving in the future, even if we've made some wrong turns in the past.

Not only does the Bible teach us this, but so does modern-day psychology.

Morgan Housel, in his bestselling book *The Psychology of Money*, highlights two extremes that people often fall into with their finances: overspending or oversaving. Both paths lead to dead ends.

Overspenders chase fleeting happiness. The thrill of a purchase quickly fades, leaving them needing the next big thing to fill the void. On the other hand, oversavers often miss out on life in the present, working long hours and trusting their growing bank accounts for security. Both approaches can leave us unfulfilled.

Housel suggests we ask one key question about our financial decisions: *"Will I regret spending this—or not spending this—someday?"*[52] This simple question helps recalibrate our choices, focusing on what truly matters.

Gerontologist (I had to look that up . . . it's a scientist who studies aging) Carl Piller, author of *30 Lessons for Living*, echoed this idea after interviewing over 100 centenarians (also looked that up . . . people who lived to be 100 years old). When asked about their regrets, not one said they wished they had earned more money. Instead, they reflected on the time they wished they had spent with loved ones, pursuing meaningful relationships and experiences.

This wisdom is a reminder: How we earn, save, and spend money shapes our lives, but it should never define them. What I found particularly interesting about Houser's perspective is how psychology encourages us to be intentional about where our money is going—both in the big picture, with an eternal perspective, and in the smaller, everyday decisions we make.

OVERFLOWING POCKETS

One thing I've never regretted doing with my money is giving it away.

In the mid-2010s, we had saved up enough money to put a pool in our backyard. Living in Florida, it seemed like the obvious choice, especially since all our neighbors had pools. But we couldn't shake the feeling that God was stirring something in our hearts, asking us to give that money to our church's renovation plans instead. The church was growing, and our renovation plans provided us an opportunity to expand our building, which we believed would help us reach more people.

After praying, we decided to forego the pool and give the money to the church. Looking back, I'm so grateful we didn't spend that money on a pool or even tuck it away into savings. By giving it to our church, combined with many more generous churchgoers, we were able to complete our renovation, expand our seating capacity, and reach so many more people.

If we'd gone ahead with the pool, I know I'd have regretted it. And honestly, when we moved a few years later, I was even more thankful we didn't invest in something we couldn't take with us. I'm not saying it's wrong if you own a pool, but for us it simply wasn't right.

Think about it: How many "former givers" do you know? Probably none. That's because giving never leaves us with regret. Instead, it aligns our hearts with God's, reminds us of His provision, and draws us closer to the people and purposes that truly matter.

Contrast that with buyer's remorse. We've all been there, purchasing something we didn't need or couldn't afford, only to feel regret almost immediately. Jesus addresses this so powerfully in Luke 6:38:

> **"Give, and it will be given to you. A good measure, pressed down, shaken together and running over, will be poured into your lap. For with the measure you use, it will be measured to you."**

In Jesus's time, grain sellers would press down and shake the grain to remove air pockets, making sure the measure was full and overflowing. This wasn't just about accuracy—it showed sincerity and fairness in how the grain was measured. When sellers operated like this, God promised blessings that would overflow into their laps. Back then, people wore robes that could fold over to create pockets in their laps, making it easy to carry those blessings.

God tells us that when we give generously and without holding back, when we "remove the air pockets" in our giving, we can trust Him to fill our lives to overflowing. These blessings aren't always financial, but they always leave us deeply fulfilled.

Rather than grabbing as much as we can now or hoarding for the future, we're called to live with gratitude for what God has already provided. Gratitude opens our eyes to blessings we might otherwise overlook and gives us the freedom to live generously.

When we recalibrate our choices, whether it's rethinking a purchase, prioritizing relationships, or giving freely, we align ourselves with God's purpose. And when we give, Jesus reminds us that God fills our lives to overflowing.

God doesn't panic when we make a wrong turn. Instead, He patiently redirects us, offering grace and guidance as we find our way back to Him. Recalibrating isn't about regret; it's about refocusing, trusting His plan, and moving forward with hearts full of gratitude and lives overflowing with His blessings—pressed down, shaken together, and running over.

PRAY DAY

Every week you will be challenged to pray about your giving. As you discern what/how to give each week, you will never be told a specific amount. Our recommendation for you is to bring all these decisions before God through prayer.

Here are the prayer steps we'll be asking you to follow each week:

1. Acknowledge that God is most generous and thank Him for His provision.

2. Ask God how you can be generous this week.

3. Listen for His direction. For specifics on how to hear God's voice, check out this blog: "3 Questions to Help You Know if You Are Hearing God's Voice."

4. Be obedient. When God is leading you to give, follow His lead and trust Him fully.

#GIVINGCHALLENGE

If you need more direction, here's a prayer you can pray this week:

Heavenly Father,

I come before You today with an open heart, asking You to guide me in my giving. You are the Ultimate Provider, and all I have comes from You. So, Lord, what would You have me give? How can my gift this week put a stop to grasping for more, but instead reflect my gratitude for You and what You have so graciously given to me?

God, I'm quieting my heart and listening for Your direction. Give me discernment to recognize Your voice now and clarity to follow where You lead.

Consider pausing in silence for a minute or two.

Lord, I choose to trust You. I will respond with obedience. I know that You see the bigger picture, that You have my best in mind, and that You will always provide for my needs. Help me to release any fear or hesitation, and to give with a joyful heart. May my giving be an act of worship that draws me closer to Your heart.

In Jesus's name,
Amen.

37/40

DAY 38

THE GREED SPIRAL

> "For God did not send his Son into the world to condemn the world, but in order that the world might be saved through him."
>
> **John 3:17 (ESV)**

Grasping for more, what the Bible classifies as greed, is everywhere. You could argue it's the top sin Jesus addressed due to how often He discussed money and its power. But although the Bible repeatedly warns about greed's consequences, this sin is often treated too cavalier, despite the extreme examples of its consequences.

None of us wake up planning to be greedy, yet greed often becomes our reality. It doesn't announce its consequences upfront or show the devastation it will cause over time. Instead, it creeps in subtly, drawing us in step by step.

Today, we'll examine the four stages of the "Greed Spiral."

To illustrate, we'll focus on the story of Achan from Joshua 7. Achan was an Israelite whose greed brought tragedy to himself, his family, and the entire nation of Israel. Achan disobeyed God's command after the battle of Jericho by secretly taking forbidden plunder and hiding it in his tent.

Let's explore how this happened and what we can learn from his mistake.

STAGE 1: I SAW

Every sin begins with a moment of seeing. Achan sinned in the aftermath of Jericho's fall. God had commanded Israel to destroy the city of Jericho and devote its treasures to Him: **"But keep away from the devoted things, so that you will not bring about your own destruction by taking any of them." Joshua 6:18a**

As the walls of Jericho fell, Achan's eyes landed on something tempting.

> **"When I saw in the plunder a beautiful robe from Babylonia, two hundred shekels of silver, and a bar of gold weighing fifty shekels . . ." Joshua 7:21a**

What Achan saw wasn't inherently sinful. Temptation often enters through the eyes, and we've all experienced moments like this. The issue isn't the first glance but what we choose to do next. Will we look away, or will we allow our eyes to linger?

Temptation is like a fisherman's lure. It doesn't show the hook; it dazzles with shiny bait, promising something good. Achan's decision to linger on what he saw set him on a path of destruction. If he had looked away, his story might have ended differently. But he didn't, and he entered the next stage.

STAGE 2: I COVETED

Being tempted isn't a sin, despite what Satan wants you to believe. But allowing the temptation to take root in our hearts is a sin.

Achan's confession continues: **"I coveted them . . ." Joshua 7:21b** What he saw with his eyes began to consume his thoughts. He imagined the robe's luxurious feel, the wealth that the silver and gold could bring. He wanted what wasn't his to take.

Coveting arises from discontentment. It's the lie that what God has provided isn't enough. For Achan, the treasures of Jericho represented security and satisfaction apart from God. His imagination ran wild, and his heart became captive to his longings.

This stage is dangerous because it's internal. No one else can see what's happening in our minds. But unchecked desire is like a spark in dry grass. It quickly spreads. As James 1:14-15 warns, **"Each person is tempted when they are dragged away by their own evil desire and enticed. Then, after desire has conceived, it gives birth to sin; and sin, when it is full-grown, gives birth to death."**

Achan's desire for material wealth overpowered his trust in God's provision. He ignored God's command, allowing his thoughts to spiral into action.

STAGE 3: I TOOK

Desire leads to action. Achan admits, **"I coveted them and took them."** Joshua 7:21b

What began as a glance turned into a decision. He reached out, took the forbidden treasures, and hid them beneath the ground in his tent. In that moment, Achan's thoughts became deeds, and his rebellion against God was complete.

Most of the egregious acts you've committed were not done immediately but involved many thoughts and smaller decisions along the way.

In a lot of experiences, the seeing and coveting could be for minutes, hours, or years, but the taking is just a millisecond. And at this point, the dam is broken.

Sin often seems small at the moment. Achan might have rationalized, "It's just a robe and some silver. No one will notice." But sin always has consequences. It ripples outward, affecting others in ways we can't predict. For Achan, his actions caused Israel's defeat at Ai, leading to the deaths of 36 soldiers. His personal sin brought collective suffering.

Achan's decision highlights how individual sin can have communal consequences. His greed disrupted God's blessing over the entire nation. Similarly, our private actions can deeply affect those around us.

STAGE 4: I HID

After taking the treasures, Achan buried them under his tent. He thought he could hide his sin, but God saw everything. When Israel faced defeat at Ai, Joshua sought the Lord, who revealed the truth: **"Israel has sinned; they have violated my covenant . . . They have taken some of the devoted things; they have stolen, they have lied, they have put them with their own possessions." Joshua 7:11**

Like Achan, we often try to cover our sins. Hidden sin festers. It weighs on our consciences and separates us from God. Proverbs 28:13 warns, **"Whoever conceals their sins does not prosper, but the one who confesses and renounces them finds mercy."**

When Achan's sin was exposed, he and his family faced judgment. They were stoned and burned, and a pile of rocks was heaped over them as a reminder to Israel of the cost of disobedience. His attempt to hide only delayed the inevitable reckoning.

BREAKING OUT OF THE SPIRAL

Achan's story shows a clear pattern of sin, but we see this elsewhere in Scripture.

The most famous king of Israel, David, followed the same spiral with a woman named Bathsheba: He saw her, coveted her, took her, and tried to hide his actions through deception and murder (2 Samuel 11-12).

At the very beginning, with the very first sin, Eve fell into this spiral too: She saw the one fruit that she was not supposed to eat, coveted it, took a bite, and then hid in shame when God confronted her (Genesis 3).

These stories remind us that the Greed Spiral is not unique to one person or time. It's a universal human struggle.

The good news is that we can escape the spiral. As Jesus said, **"For God did not send his Son into the world to condemn the world, but in order that the world might be saved through him." John 3:17 (ESV)** Through Jesus, we're offered grace and redemption, no matter where we are in the spiral.

We don't have to stay trapped in the spiral of seeing, coveting, taking, and hiding. God provides a way out at every stage. When temptation appears, we can look away and fix our eyes on Jesus. When covetous thoughts arise, we can combat them with gratitude and contentment. If we've sinned, we can confess, repent, find forgiveness, and stop hiding.

As 1 John 1:9 promises, **"If we confess our sins, he is faithful and just and will forgive us our sins and purify us from all unrighteousness."**

Greed is powerful, but God's grace is greater. Wherever you find yourself in the spiral, whether you've just seen the bait or you've taken it and are full-on hiding, God invites you to turn back to Him. Confess your sins, trust in Jesus, and walk in the freedom He offers.

#GIVINGCHALLENGE

CHALLENGE

PREP DAY

Yesterday you prayed about a gift that you can give away. Tomorrow you will be encouraged to give your gift away. Write down the gift you are feeling led to give tomorrow. You can write the amount and who you'd like to give the gift to. It can be a person, an organization, or your local church.

AMOUNT: _____

RECIPIENT: _____

As you write your potential gift down, pause and pray. In your prayer, ask God these three questions.

① Is my gift generous?

② Is my gift sacrificial?

③ Is my gift obedient?

- If the answers are "yes," then ask God to guide you in staying faithful to your decision.

- If the answers are "maybe," consider if God is asking you to give more.

- If the answers are "no," practice writing a higher number until you feel confident that what you are giving is generous, sacrificial, and obedient.

As you prepare to let go of some of the resources that God has given you to help someone else's life today, know that you are getting ready to reflect the love of Jesus, and His love changes everything!

38/40

DAY 39

SOWING SEED

> "Still other seed fell on good soil. It came up and yielded a crop, a hundred times more than was sown."
> Luke 8:8a

In December of 2020, a man pulled up to a Dairy Queen drive-up window and asked if he could pay for his meal as well as the stranger's meal behind him. Of course, the cashier said, "Yes." Out of gratitude for the gift, the woman behind him decided to step into the generosity movement as well, and she paid for the car behind her. This went on and on and on for two and a half days. In total, more than 900 consecutive meals were paid for, amounting to more than $10,000.[53]

When you are a recipient of generosity, your gratitude for the gift fosters a desire to get into the generosity game as well.

Jesus made a similar point—generosity multiplies—in his famous Parable of the Sower. This was one of His many agricultural examples to help His hearers understand what the Kingdom of God is like.

> **While a large crowd was gathering and people were coming to Jesus from town after town, he told this parable:** "A farmer went out to sow his seed. As he was scattering the seed, some fell along the path; it was trampled on, and the birds ate it up. Some fell on rocky ground, and when it came up, the plants withered because they had no moisture. Other seed fell among thorns, which grew up with it and choked the plants. Still other seed fell on good soil. It came up and yielded a crop, a hundred times more than was sown." Luke 8:4-8a

The Parable of the Sower also is one of the rare parables that Jesus explained to the disciples. The seed is the Word of God, and Jesus reminds us that He has planted the Good News within everybody. How it is received is another thing.

Some of the seed falls on bad soil, while some falls on good soil. Some of it falls on soil that will even produce a hundredfold. The point of the story is that just as God has made His Good News available to us, we too are called to plant the seed of Good News in anybody and everybody today.

The word "seed" is still used today in many Christian circles—not just to describe the Good News of Jesus, but also our giving. Just as God calls us to share the Good News of Jesus with others, He also invites us to share our resources. When we share the Kingdom of God with others, whether it's through our words, actions, or resources, it gives God the opportunity to work powerfully.

Planting our seed requires us to loosen our grip on what God has given to us. When we drop that seed, we should realize at times that it will fall on rocky soil. Other times, it might produce a good return initially but fizzle out later. But sometimes, as Jesus said, the seed we sow may produce a hundredfold. In the case of Dairy Queen in Brainerd, Minnesota, it produced 900-fold.

I don't know if we are supposed to look at his example purely mathematically, but the principle still applies. Generosity multiplies.

I LIKE GIVING

I met Drew Formsma at a conference and was immediately captured by his youth and his passion for generosity. I was also inspired to learn his story.

At the age of 14, Drew was already speaking at churches and conferences, talking about the joy that comes from living the generous life. Drew's parents modeled this type of living. His dad, Brad, formed a company called "I Like Giving," and now alongside Drew, they take the generosity message all over the world to inspire people to live more generous lives.

They do it primarily through stories.

The best way to truly capture someone's heart for generosity is to share stories. People can argue with statistics, opinions, and beliefs, but it's hard to argue with someone's story. So, together, Brad and Drew went on a journey to highlight stories of those who give generously.

One of their videos that really moved me is called "I Like Car." It tells the story of a woman named Catherine who worked at a local bread company. Catherine was struggling and needed a reliable car. She had been saving up for one, but her savings just weren't enough. Then, something incredible happened. Instead of holding onto her money, she came across a widow who was in need. Catherine decided to give the widow all $5,000 she had saved. It left her with nothing, but her heart was full.

Enter Pete and Debbie Ochs, regular customers at the bread shop who had come to know Catherine and her story. Grateful for all that God had done in their life, they were committed to living a generous life. So, when they heard about her act of generosity, they felt compelled to do something extraordinary for her. They didn't just want to replace the money she'd given away. Instead, they decided to surprise her with a brand-new SUV, and they kept the whole thing a secret.

The day they came into the bread shop, Catherine was happy to see them as usual because they were friends. But this time, Pete and Debbie couldn't wait to share their big surprise. They brought her outside and handed her the keys to her brand-new SUV. Catherine was stunned and overjoyed. She never imagined something like this could happen to her.

GENEROSITY IS
CONTAGIOUS,
FUN, AND
LIFE-GIVING.

#GIVINGCHALLENGE

The joy didn't stop with Catherine. Pete and Debbie were equally overjoyed to see her happiness. It was a beautiful moment of generosity coming full circle, showing how giving can spark joy not just for the receiver but for the giver too.[54]

Generosity is contagious, fun, and life-giving.

Catherine's story reminds us that generosity begets generosity. She gave sacrificially to help someone in need, and while she didn't expect anything in return, she was blessed in an unexpected and amazing way. It doesn't always work out like this. We don't always see a financial blessing after we give. But one thing is certain: Giving fills your life with joy. And that's a greater reward in itself!

There are small, medium, and big opportunities to be generous every day. Whether you give a couple of bucks to help someone pay for a meal or thousands of dollars to buy someone in need of a new SUV, when you live in gratitude for what God has given to you, you can't help but see people and opportunities all around you.

My encouragement for you is if you really want to test whether generosity is as joy-filled, fun, and exciting as Jesus says it is, then live it out for yourself.

Sow the seed of generosity, show the world your heart is devoted to God, and you will experience for yourself the generous life that God so lovingly gave to you!

CHALLENGE

GIVE DAY

Today you are being challenged to give your fifth and final gift of these 40 days. This gift will allow you to let go of greed and instead live with gratitude.

All this week you have studied how greed fights against gratitude. You have assessed how Jesus gave to help us today. You have learned how we, too, can combat greed with gratitude. Out of gratitude for what God has given to us, you are being called to give a gift today that could truly impact someone's life.

Led by God, let go of greed and live with gratitude. After giving today's gift, give thanks that God allowed you to make a difference in someone else's life.

39/40

DAY 40

GENEROSITY SAVES LIVES

"Freely you have received; freely give."

Matthew 10:8b

WHEN STUFF OWNS YOU

How much would you pay for extra legroom on an airplane?

The Economist recently asked this question, and the average amount that people said they would pay for the comfort was $12. But when asked how much they would need to be paid to give up the extra legroom that they paid $12 for, they required an average of $39.[55]

The inconsistency is revealing. Psychologists call this the Endowment Effect. It's the tendency for us to overvalue things we own. It explains why we are so unwilling to give something up once we have ownership of it.

At first, the researchers thought this was a classic case of loss aversion, where we feel the pain of losing something more strongly than the pleasure of gaining something. But the simple truth is this: We value something more *simply because it is ours.*

The more we have, the more we value it, and the more we want to hold onto it.

We don't naturally realize the power and the hold that our possessions have over us. We think it's wise to own as much stuff as we can, and before we realize it, our stuff begins to own us. Think about how much time you spend in your day, week, month, or year caring, tending, and taking care of your stuff. If our strategy is just to get more, we'll never be satisfied.

There is a better way to live.

Rather than grasping for more and becoming close-fisted when you get it, God invites you to live open-handed, to see all of life as a gift meant to be shared with others. Jesus offers this truth, which radically opposes the grasping nature of greed: **"Freely you have received; freely give." Matthew 10:8b**

This verse is not just a command; it's an invitation to embrace a greater life of gratitude and generosity.

God's blessings are meant to "get to us" and also "go through us."

GRATITUDE DEFEATS ANXIETY

One way we can ensure that God's blessings go through us is to get in a regular practice of gratitude each and every day. Not only does gratitude put us in a better posture toward our finances, but it affects our mental well-being too.

We live in a world filled with anxiety. So much of the anxiety we experience is due to our incessant drive for more or to keep up with those around us. The answers for how to combat anxiety are all over the map. Therapy, healthy eating, exercise, breathing techniques, and talking about your feelings are some of the top ways to combat this epidemic. All of them are just fine, and there's probably great wisdom in them.

But, so too, is the simple practice of waking up every day and being grateful for what you have. Did you know that psychology teaches us that it's impossible for gratitude and anxiety to exist simultaneously in the brain?[56] If you woke up every morning, or conversely, went to bed each night, and wrote down three things you were grateful for, how much do you think your perspective would shift?

Gratitude transforms our perspective. It reminds us that everything we have is a gift from God, freely given by His grace. And when we fully grasp the depth of His generosity toward us, not only are we healthier, but our hearts naturally overflow with a desire to give freely to others. Gratitude isn't just a feeling; it's a practice that shapes our attitudes and actions, enabling us to combat the destructive force of greed.

Gratitude fuels generosity.

And, you never know what kind of difference God's blessings given through you to others may make in somebody's life.

GENEROSITY SAVES LIVES

A young woman at the end of her rope was pleading with God as she was going through the drive-thru lane at a fast-food restaurant. She said, "God, if you are real, you need to send me a sign now." She had already decided that unless God intervened, this would be her last day on Earth. She ordered what was going to be her last meal and followed the car in front of her to the pick-up window.

Driving the car ahead of her happened to be a pastor who had just launched an "Acts of Kindness" challenge at his church. Alongside this challenge, he gave ideas for how people could be kind to people every day, with a particular emphasis on being generous.

Some ideas included in the list were things like:

1. Pay for someone's gas.
2. Mow someone's yard for free.
3. Pay for someone's fast food meal behind you in the drive-thru.

#GIVINGCHALLENGE

4 Leave a big tip for your server at a restaurant.

5 Help someone you know who is struggling financially.

He was doing his best to encourage those who came to his church to live with gratitude and practice generosity, even if it's in little ways, each and every day.

With the acts of kindness, he also handed out little business-size cards that looked a bit like this:

Later that day, as he was going through the drive-thru, he decided to pay for the person's lunch behind him. He instructed the cashier not to take their payment and to give them the acts of kindness card along with the lunch. The cashier agreed, handed him his lunch, and the pastor drove off. He was happy to be generous in a small way. Little did he know how this small gift would make such a huge difference.

The woman pulled up and started to get out her cash to pay for the meal. Suddenly, the cashier said, "Your meal is free today. The man ahead of you paid for it, and he wanted you to have this." The cashier handed the woman the card, and she read the phrase on the card, "Something extra to show you God loves you."

At the perfect time, right when this woman needed to see God's love, it was on display through a pastor, a card, and about a $10 meal. That was all she needed to turn her life around. She would later find the pastor and thank him for his act of kindness that literally saved her life.[57]

The generosity of God, to give His Son to you, followed by the generosity of the Son, who gave His life for you, is what saved your soul. Because He was generous to you, we can be generous to others.

It just might help save someone's life. It might even save your life.

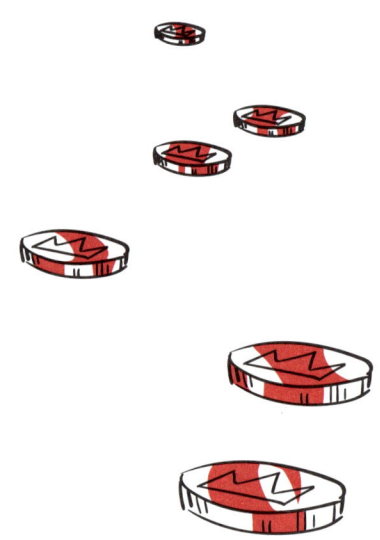

CHALLENGE

WRAP-UP DAY

Today, as we wrap up the Giving Today week, I pray that you are starting to see more and more opportunities each and every day to be generous. Spend some time reflecting on the gift you gave, and how you can keep trading greed for gratitude.

If you gave yesterday, how did it feel?

_____
_____

What would it look like to permanently trade greed for gratitude in your life?

_____
_____

What was one major takeaway, feeling, or lesson that you received from this week's devotions and challenges?

_____
_____

40/40

THE FINAL CHALLENGE

> "Now that you know these things, you will be blessed if you do them."
>
> **John 13:17**

You did it. Forty days of learning, stretching, giving, and growing. It hasn't been easy. At times, it's probably been uncomfortable. But here you are—on the other side of *Giving Challenge*. And I hope you're not the same person anymore.

You've learned that generosity is not a moment—it's a lifestyle. A generous life doesn't begin or end with this book. This was only the launchpad. Now, it's time to take the leap and let generosity become a defining rhythm in your life.

So, before we look ahead, pause for a moment. Think back on your journey. Reflect on the five gifts you gave over these past weeks. Each one was an expression of your heart, an act of faith, and a step toward the generous life that God calls us to live. What stories came from those gifts? What did they reveal about God, about others, about you?

With your generous gifts, you traded the world's ways of using money for God's way. Which was easiest? Most challenging?

- Was it learning to trade comfort for contentment?
- Was it trusting God with the idea of stewardship?
- Was it breaking the grip of scarcity with a new mindset of abundance?

- Was it living with obedience to God and letting go of your control?

- Was it expressing gratitude instead of always grasping for more?

What were your five biggest takeaways? You can review your weekly takeaways from the challenges on Days 12, 19, 26, 33, and 40. Write them down again. Own them.

1. _____
2. _____
3. _____
4. _____
5. _____

These are the seeds God planted in your heart during your 40 days. Please don't leave them buried in the past. Continue to do something with them.

So, here's your final challenge:

Choose one way to grow in your generosity moving forward.

Maybe it's committing to a recurring gift. Maybe it's setting a "finish line" for your lifestyle and giving the rest away. Maybe it's increasing your giving percentage this year or making your largest gift ever. Maybe it's teaching your children or grandchildren to live generously. Maybe it's reviewing your estate planning to ensure that your generosity flows now and continues to bless others and build God's Kingdom after you pass.

You choose. Just make it personal. Make it intentional. Make it real.

And once you choose it, write it down. Pray over it. Share it with your accountability partner or someone you love. And most importantly—act on it.

Because now you know:

Giving isn't just something you do. It's someone you become.

In our final red letters, Jesus once again uses that Greek word "*makarios*," meaning blessed, most happy, and fortunate.

Most happy are the ones who do what Jesus calls us to do.

The world needs more generous people. Your church, city, neighbors, and family need to see what it looks like when someone takes Jesus at His word and gives as He did.

Not only does the world need your generosity, but you do too. If you call yourself a Christian, it's time to truly live according to His ways. When you do, you'll be most happy.

So, what's your next generous step? Write it down.

This is the one next step I'm committing to:

_____

Let's walk boldly into the life Jesus has called us to live.

This is not the end. It's just the beginning.

As Jesus promised: **Makarios.**
Blessed are those who do what He says.

JOIN THE RED LETTER COMMUNITY.

You don't have to follow Jesus alone! Commit today to a lifelong pursuit to follow Jesus.

Jump into the FREE Red Letter Community for ongoing discipleship challenges, brand new podcasts featuring world-class disciples, Jesus-centered blogs, Bible reading plans, and much, much more. Join today at:

WWW.REDLETTERCOMMUNITY.COM.

ABOUT THE AUTHOR

Zach Zehnder is a husband, father, pastor, author, and public speaker. He and his wife, Allison, live in Omaha, Nebraska, with their two sons, Nathan and Brady.

Zach's life mission is to challenge people of all ages to become greater followers of Jesus. He is the Founder and President of Red Letter Living, author of the bestselling *Red Letter Challenge*, and host of *The Red Letter Disciple* podcast. To date, he has written or co-authored eleven books that have helped people grow as disciples of Jesus.

In addition to leading Red Letter Living, Zach currently serves as the Multisite Director and a Teaching Pastor at King of Kings in Omaha.

Zach is an experienced public speaker with a passion for making Jesus's name great. To book him for your conference, church, or event, go to:

WWW.REDLETTERCHALLENGE.COM/ZACH.

ENDNOTES

1. "The Ultimate List of Charitable Giving Statistics for 2024." *Nonprofits Source*. Web. Accessed 19 March 2025.
2. "Church Giving Stats and Strategies for Adapting to New Trends." *Vanco*. Web. Accessed 19 March 2025.
3. Anderson, Max. "Remembering Tim Keller: The heart is an idol factory." *Premier Unbelievable*. Accessed 19 March 2025.
4. Keller, Tim. "Tim Keller—The Gospel, Grace, and Giving." Vimeo. Web. Accessed 19 March 2025.
5. Dunn, Elizabeth and Dr. Michael Norton. *Happy Money: The Science of Happier Spending*. Simon & Schuster, 2013, p. xviii.
6. Twenge, Jean M. "The Sad State of Happiness in the United States and the Role of Digital Media." *World Happiness Report*. Web. Accessed 19 March 2025.
7. Dunn, Elizabeth and Dr. Michael Norton. *Happy Money: The Science of Happier Spending*. Simon & Schuster, 2013, p. 113.
8. "Life, Liberty, and the Pursuit of Happiness." Wikipedia. Web. Accessed 19 March 2025.
9. The first recorded words of Jesus are found in Matthew 4 and 5. In Matthew 5:3-11, the word "*makarios*" is translated as happy or blessed and used nine times.
10. Pokluda, Jonathan. "Book Club: Part 3, The Cure for Greed." Open Network. Web. Accessed 19 March 2025.
11. Jenkinson, Clay S. "Too Much Stuff: Americans and Their Storage Units." *Governing*. Web. Accessed 19 March 2025.
12. "The 10% Pledge." *Giving What We Can*. Web. Accessed 19 March 2025.
13. Roach, David. "In Church Planting, More Money Means More People." *Christianity Today*. Web. Accessed 19 March 2025.
14. Keller, Tim. "Tim Keller—The Gospel, Grace, and Giving." Vimeo. Web. Accessed 19 March 2025.
15. "How Many Ads Does a Person See in a Day." *Zippia*. Web. Accessed 19 March 2025.
16. Keller, Erin. "'White Lotus' fuels huge tourism spike for Sicily." *NY Post*. Web. Accessed 19 March 2025.
17. Jones, Nona. *Killing Comparison*. Zondervan, 2022, p. 133.
18. DeJohn, Jaclyn. "Salary Needed to Live Comfortably – 2024 Study." *SmartAsset*. Web. Accessed 19 March 2025.
19. Alcorn, Randy. "Joy is Found in Being Rich in Good Works: Tom and Bree Hsieh's Story." *Eternal Perspective Ministries*. Web. Accessed 19 March 2025.
20. Cortines, John, and Gregory Baumer. *True Riches*. Thomas Nelson, 2019, p. 51.
21. Zehnder, Zach, and Allison Zehnder. *Red Letter Advent*. Red Letter Living, 2024, p. 101.
22. Cortines, John, and Gregory Baumer. *True Riches*. Thomas Nelson, 2019, p. 58.
23. Burge, Ryan. "Does Religion Generate Higher Levels of Self-Reported Well Being?" *Graphs About Religion*. Web. Accessed 19 March 2025.
24. Lewis, C.S. *Mere Christianity*. HarperCollins, 2009, pp. 55-56.
25. Props to Pastor Craig Groeschel who mentioned this in one of his past sermons.
26. Elliott, Ed. "Did Jesus Talk More about Hell than He Did Heaven?" Facebook. Web. Accessed 19 March 2025.
27. Cortines, John, and Gregory Baumer. *True Riches*. Thomas Nelson, 2019, p. 104.

28. Lazar, Shawn. "40 References to Rewards in the Teaching of Jesus." *GES*. Web. Accessed 19 March 2025.
29. Alcorn, Randy. *The Treasure Principle: Unlocking the Secret of Joyful Giving*. Multnomah, 2017, p.11.
30. ChatGPT, 12.7.24, OpenAI, https://chat.openai.com. Prompt: Write me a modern day story no more than two paragraphs using as many Gen Z words and slogans as possible.
31. Tverberg, Lois. *Walking in the Dust of Rabbi Jesus*. Zondervan. Kindle Edition, 2012, pp. 69-70.
32. Zehnder, Zach. *Forgiving Challenge: A 40-Day Life-Changing Journey to Freedom*. Red Letter Living, 2021, p. 33.
33. Easter, Michael. *Scarcity Brain*. Rodale Books, 2023, pp. 9-17.
34. Ibid, 49.
35. Ibid, 5.
36. Ibid, 7.
37. "Sasha Berscheid on Gaining Victory Over Alcoholism and Discovering Her Purpose through Serving Single Moms." Red Letter Living. Web. Accessed 19 March 2025.
38. "Peter Greer on Devoting His Life to Eradicating Poverty and How to Flip from a Scarcity to Abundance Mindset." Red Letter Living. Web. Accessed 19 March 2025.
39. Comer, John Mark. "There is More Joy in Giving than Receiving." RightNow Media. Web. Accessed 19 March 2025.
40. *State of the Bible USA 2024*. American Bible Society. PDF. Accessed 19 March 2025, p. 178.
41. Zehnder, Zach. *Serving Challenge: A 40-Day Life-Changing Journey to Serve Like Jesus*. Red Letter Living, 2023, pp. 124-125
42. Clear, James. *Atomic Habits*. Penguin, 2018, p. 27.
43. Zehnder, Zach. *Being Challenge: A 40-Day Challenge to be Like Jesus*. Red Letter Living, 2020, p. 21.
44. Cortines, John, and Gregory Baumer. *God and Money*. Rose Publishing Inc, 2016, p. 34.
45. "Handful of Rice—Mizoram, India." CofEWinchester. YouTube. Web. Accessed 19 March 2025.
46. Alcorn, Randy. *Money, Possessions, and Eternity*. Tyndale House, 2003, p.174.
47. Batterson, Mark. *The Circle Maker*. Zondervan, 2016, pp. 59-62.
48. *Wall Street*, directed by Oliver Stone (1987; Century City, CA: Twentieth Century Fox, 2007), DVD.
49. Oliver, Mary. "Mary Oliver Quotes." Goodreads. Web. Accessed 19 March 2025.
50. Tyson, Jon. "Seven Deadly Sins: Greed." Apple Podcasts. Web. Accessed 19 March 2025.
51. "Jemar Tisby on the History of Racism, How Race, Religion, Politics Are All Tied Together, and Developing a Plan to Fight Racism." Red Letter Living. Web. Accessed 19 March 2025.
52. Andrew Huberman. "Morgan Housel: Understand & Apply the Psychology of Money to Gain Greater Happiness." YouTube. Web. Accessed 19 March 2025.
53. "More than 900 cars 'pay-it-forward' in random act of drive-through kindness." *BBC*. Web. Accessed 19 March 2025.
54. "I Like Car." I Like Giving. YouTube. Web. Accessed 19 March 2025.
55. B.R. "Who owns the space between reclining airline seats?" *The Economist*. Web. Accessed 19 March 2025.
56. Chowdbury, Madhuleena R. "The Neuroscience of Gratitude and Effects on the Brain." *Positive Psychology*. Web. Accessed 19 March 2025.
57. "Acts of Kindness." Church of the Highlands. Web. Accessed 19 March 2025.

APPENDIX

FIFTEEN GENEROSITY PRACTICES
TO CONSIDER

1. **Tithe First**

   A tithe means giving away 10 percent of your income. If you haven't developed this habit yet, consider making your local church the first place you give, investing in God's work in your community.

2. **Add 2 Percent Annually**

   Each year, review your charitable giving as a percentage of your total income (your tax return can help). Whatever your current level, challenge yourself to increase it by 2 percent annually for as long as possible.

3. **Use the Regular, Random, and Radical Framework**

   One donor created this framework to guide a lifestyle of intentional generosity:

   - **Regular:** A planned gift (often more than a tithe) given routinely to your church.
   - **Random:** Smaller, flexible gifts given monthly—to freewill offerings, galas, or individuals in need.
   - **Radical:** A sacrificial, significant gift given annually, planned or spontaneous, that stretches faith and impacts lives.

4. **Make Your Church Your Largest Monthly Payment**

   Review your monthly expenses and consider this question: Could your largest monthly payment be your gift to the local church? This reorients your heart and priorities around God's Kingdom.

5. **Annual Clean-Out**

   Once a year, choose a month to go through your home. Any items unused in the last year? Donate them to someone in need or to an organization that can bless others.

6. **Practice the Big Tip**

   Whenever you eat out, add an extra $10, $20, $50, or even $100—above and beyond your regular tip—depending on your financial ability. This unexpected generosity can powerfully impact someone's day.

7. **Donate Your Tax Refund**

   If you receive a sizable federal or state refund, consider giving it away instead of spending it. Support a cause that is near to your heart or meets a need in your church or community.

8. **The Thanks-Give-Ing Gift**

   Each Thanksgiving, give your kids, grandkids, or close friends a set amount of money and challenge them to give it away during the Christmas season. Follow up with them to hear how their gift made a difference.

9. **Review Your Estate Plan Annually**

   Once a year, take time to review your estate and financial legacy. Ask two key questions:

   1. Is your security rooted in your net worth—or in God?
   2. Will your resources continue to support Kingdom impact after you're gone?

   After prayerful reflection, consider how your estate can reflect your values and faith. Look for opportunities to greater impact ministries, churches, and individuals both now and long after your lifetime.

10. **Follow the Old Testament Giving Model**

    Practice the "three tithes" described in the Old Testament and give 23.3 percent of your income each year:

    - 10 percent to your local church,
    - 10 percent to other God-honoring causes,
    - 3.3 percent to support the poor (which could be given as a 10-percent lump sum every three years).

11. **Make a December Stock Donation**

    At year's end, review your financial portfolio. Consider donating appreciated stock to your church or favorite ministry—this helps avoid capital gains tax and maximizes your impact.

12. Pool Money with Others

Gather a few friends or your small group, pool your money, and decide together how to bless someone in need—perhaps a single parent, missionary, or struggling family. Sharing in acts of generosity with others multiplies the joy.

13. Live Below Your Means

Choose one or two areas of your life where you will intentionally live below your means. This creates financial margin and reminds you to rely on God. It could be driving an older car, cutting back on eating out, or limiting subscriptions.

14. Create a "Blessing Fund"

Set aside a small amount of money each month—$25, $50, $100, or whatever you can—as a designated fund for spontaneous generosity. When a need arises or God puts someone on your heart, you'll be ready to act immediately.

15. Give on Payday

Make it a habit to give every time you receive income. Whether it's a paycheck, bonus, or unexpected gift, practice giving a portion right away to remind yourself that everything comes from God and belongs to Him.

The Red Letter Disciple is a podcast to help you become the greatest disciple of Jesus that you can possible be! Learn more at:

WWW.REDLETTERPODCAST.COM

Subscribe or Follow:

Apple Podcasts   YouTube   Spotify

READY FOR THE NEXT CHALLENGE?

40 DAYS TO BECOME A GREATER DISCIPLE OF JESUS

EXPERIENCE RAPID GROWTH IN YOUR RELATIONSHIP WITH GOD IN ONLY 40 DAYS

EXPERIENCE THE FREEDOM OF GOD IN JUST 40 DAYS!

FIND MORE FULFILLMENT THAN YOU EVER THOUGHT POSSIBLE IN JUST 40 DAYS!

FIND OUT MORE AT
WWW.REDLETTERCHALLENGE.COM